Time and the River

Michael Mulheirn —

Time and the River

A Memoir

Michael Freeland

Periploi Press / NASHVILLE

Published by Periploi Press
Nashville, Tennessee

ISBN 978-0-9830-1150-7
Library of Congress Control Number: 2010937681

Frontispiece: Murphy, N.C. Photo by Ellen Freeland
This book is printed on acid-free paper
made from 30% post-consumer recycled content.
Printed in the United States by Thomson-Shore, Inc.
Designed by Dariel Mayer

ALSO BY MICHAEL FREELAND:
Blood River to Berlin:
The World War II Journal
of an Army Medic

Dedicated with love
to these strong women:

Wilby Lee Murphy Freeland, my mother
Amy Flora Meeks Elmore, my mother-in-law
Flora Ellen Elmore Freeland

It is a long road to the end of wonder,
and some of us never reach it,
but there is the joy of trying.
    —Harriet Simpson Arnow
    Seedtime on the Cumberland

I am the north wind.
My spirit rides these dark hills
Listening, seeking, and remembering.
And I am the river.
Come look at me. Be still and listen to my song.
Come stay with me, and I will be your friend.
    —Mike Freeland

Contents

CONTENTS

Time and the River

First blush of sun
Paints the eastern sky
Holding still the early
Light.
Waiting its time,
Waiting to mark the morning.
The world waits
Silent.
Now comes the morning fire
Burning wet fog
Against the sky
And from the silent trees
Along the river.

I walk on toward what I remember as the Tennessee River, now a part of Kentucky Lake. Early light is starting to break through the trees and fog from the lake. For me, early morning is the best time for walking and for thinking. For planning my day. But most important, I find a healing energy, almost a spiritual quality, from the early morning quiet, the energy from the trees, the water, and the wind, all of the mysteries of nature.

I've come to believe that time and place largely determine who we are and who we become. If this is true, people who live in this magic valley are truly blessed.

My story began on a wet cold May morning in 1924, in the front room of the Freeland home place, not far from here where my grandparents lived. I was the first child born to young parents Wilby Lee Murphy and Mason Noel Freeland, and for the first six years of my life, the only child. I was free to roam the woods and fields completely alone. Before I learned to read and love books, I learned to read woods signs and to love nature: the silence and smell of woods after rain; the way the sky looks at sunset or break of day; the clear call of bobwhites and whippoorwills; the chorus of singing frogs and peepers in the marshes.

The Freeland home place is near a branch feeding Blood River and the Tennessee. I thought for a long time it was the center of the world until my mother told me I could throw a leaf or a chip into the branch flowing by our cabin and it would float all the way to a mysterious place called New Orleans. Then I began to dream and wonder about a larger world.

Today I'm reading *Last Child in the Woods* by Richard Louv. Louv writes:

Nature inspires creativity in a child by demanding visualization and full use of the senses. Given a chance a child will bring the confusion of the world to the woods, wash it in the creek, and turn it over to see what lives on the unseen side of that confusion. Nature can frighten a child, too, and this fright serves a purpose. In nature, a child finds freedom, fantasy, and privacy: A place distant from the adult world, a separate peace.

I'm one of the blessed. I find peace on my silent walks and I'm like the child in the woods turning over rocks to find what's there.

Where I walk today was known by the early settlers as the mouth of Sandy, and by the natives before them as the Land of Many Waters. History records it as the Jackson (or Chickasaw) Purchase. It is bounded on the east by the Tennessee River, on the west by the

Sunset at Pickwick Landing State Park. Photo by Ellen Freeland.

Mississippi, and on the north by the Ohio and said to be the smallest area in the world bordered by three such mighty streams.

The Tennessee and Mississippi are almost parallel to each other, averaging in their courses a distance of about 100 miles apart; yet by some magic of nature, the Tennessee runs north and the Mississippi runs south. As if this is not strange enough, the Tennessee empties into the Ohio whose direction of flow is southwest. I think of all this and shake my head in wonder. I sense the presence of the dark brooding river. I think, old river, if only you could talk, what secrets you could tell.

"What was life like in the long ago?" I'd ask, "and can you tell me why prosperous families like George and James Freeland, George Buchanan, General Robertson, the Greers, Porters, Houstons, and all the rest would pull up stakes, sell out, and leave their comfortable homes in communities where they were known, respected, and loved, to head off for a hardship I can't even imagine?"

[3]

Human nature being what it is, I'd ask about my families first—
and tell me please about that remarkable voyage down the river on
a flatboat from Kingsport (February 27, 1780) to the big salt lick
(Nashville) on the Cumberland, down the Tennessee by way of
Muscle Shoals, ending here at Paris Landing. Tell me, old river,
were these permanent settlers the first to see the shoreline in Henry
County?

The river is silent, but in my imagination I hear again the shrieks
of small boat horns, the low commanding bellow of the steamers,
the excited shouts of men and women, and the cries of children.

I think "permanent settlers," forgetting for a moment that families have always lived and prospered in these lush green valleys and
rolling hills. And how long is always? As far back as oral history
can recall. And how did our ancient red-skinned ancestors live?
They lived out their allotted time as they wished, simple lives, close
to the land and to nature. They were born free and they lived free
until one day the white skinned invaders came from across the broad
waters.

> When the Indian passed in dignity disturbing
> nothing and leaving nature as he found her with
> nothing to record his passage except a foot print
> or a broken twig, the white man plundered and
> wasted and shouted, frightening the silence with
> his great braying laughter and his curses.
> John Joseph Matthews, "Wah'Kon-Tah"

I'm in a writer's workshop at Paris Landing State Park in Buchanan, Tennessee, reviewing some old poems and letters I happened upon a few years ago while rummaging through Dad's shop. I found the wooden army footlocker I thought I'd lost, holding a treasure chest of half-forgotten memories. Every letter and picture, every souvenir, a captured black and red Nazi flag, paratrooper boots, Eisenhower jacket: every item alive, waiting with its own story to tell.

I'm supposed to be writing, but I'm mostly walking with my memories that come and go—soon to be forgotten. So far my effort has been journaling and picking up rocks and arrowheads. I write for a while, read what I've written, wad up the pages, and throw them away. I'd rather give blood. Yet I write some more because I must. Which come to think of it is a good rule: Don't write anything unless you must.

One of my teachers, Kentucky writer Harriet Simpson Arnow, wrote in *Seedtime on the Cumberland* "when the old storytellers die and rats and mice have had their way, the little things of ordinary people will be lost." However I believe there are no ordinary people. Scratch deep enough and long enough you'll find a story. Dig deep enough and you'll find treasure.

I'm from a long line of storytellers. My mother told her stories in song from the English and Irish ballads along with songs of the depression and Jimmy Rogers songs of hoboes and tramps. I've listened to the masters—Pap, Uncle Hall, Aunt Zella—weave their word magic as they told their tales.

Everyone has a story to tell. Without story there is nothing to bind us together and point the way. Without story there is no religion, civilization, history, or culture. "Stories and myths," writes Karen Armstrong in *A Short History of Myth*, "reflect and shape our lives—they explore our narratives that remind us of what it means to be human."

The storyteller is like the lamplighter of old who, each evening at early dusk, walked through the town lighting the street lamps so that others could follow his light and find their way. Without the light we are lost. Without the story it is as though nothing happened.

Hard Times

It's best to treat people nice, but some
people learn the hard way.
. . .
There's not ever enough time to do all that
needs to be done. Life keeps getting
in the way.

                      Chester Murphy

Chet and I still talk about our hobo days although our adventures lasted less than a few weeks in the summer of 1940. I was 16; Chester, Mom's younger brother, just two months older, but still old enough and big enough to seem like a big brother. Looking back to those hard depression years, I notice that our tales with each telling have become somewhat more romantic, exciting, and innocent. Yet Chet insists even the made up parts are all true.

On this spring night Chet and I are camped in a hobo jungle just outside Cairo, Illinois, one of my favorite towns ever since I read Mark Twain's books about life on the river. Six hobos altogether, Chet, me, and four others, all huddle around a crackling fire sharing a pot of beans with rabbit stew and coffee. I hear a boat's mournful horn from far down the river, watch as it draws closer following its searchlight through the mist and darkness. For a moment I feel a wave of homesickness, yet today has been one of our best ones. We've come all the way from St. Louis. "Not bad," Chet says. "Not bad at all. Stick with me, Bub, I'll show you some country. Tomorrow? Beats me. Like the Bible says, let tomorrow take care of itself."

"One nice thing about this life," Chet says, "wake up when you want to and catch the next train coming through no matter which way it's going. Or if it fits your fancy, stay another day and fish or maybe walk into town. Knock on just about any door, show the lady of the house your Bible and get a hand out. Never fails."

I'm tired but happy. From the river and the woods I hear familiar night sounds, a chorus of peepers, frogs and an occasional whip-poorwill. Just when I'm starting to nod off, I see one of the older men, the one called Big Red, staring at Chet and me. *What*, I think. What's this? I nudge Chet.

Big Red stands, stretches, stares straight at Chet, "Us boys here have found you both guilty of trespassing," he says. "Our kangaroo court's met and you owe the court money."

"How do you figure that, Mister?" Chet asks.

"I'm the judge. This here is the jury." He points to the grinning men sitting around the fire. "You boys pay up, ain't gonna be no trouble."

"I'm not paying nobody nothin'," Chet says.

I feel the same way, it's not fair, not that we have much—less than three dollars between us.

"Well, boys, have it your own way," Red pulls a long bladed knife, lurches toward Chet. "Have it your own way, Hon."

I feel a cold chill on my neck—colder than the wind. But Chet doesn't run. Cool as everything like he's been practicing in his mind, he snatches a half-burned two by four from the fire in one motion and swings it like a baseball bat. Red is totally surprised. Blinded by smoke, he catches the full force of the two by four flush in his face. I hear the crack like a rifle shot. Big Red spins backward spitting blood and teeth. Chet braces, waiting for another charge that doesn't come. Instead Red takes off running down the railroad tracks toward town holding his bloody face.

Not one of the men sitting by the fire has said a word or missed a bite.

Chet Murphy, age 18, U.S. Navy boot camp, Great Lakes Naval Training Station, Chicago, 1942.

Like Chet says it's best to treat people nice, but some people learn hard. Sometimes there's no other choice.

Hobo camps are almost always quiet, peaceful. A gathering of sad faced jobless men and boys sitting and sleeping around an open fire sharing whatever there is to share. Maybe some stew, some tobacco and if you're lucky some coffee and home brew. We sit around the fire saying little yet finding silent support and comfort from one another.

Problem is camping and catching trains can be habit forming, like money. The more you get the more you want. You hear the lonely whistle of a freight train you're ready to jump on. Don't matter which way it's going. Just to stay on the go. There's no work, no reason to stay—just go.

A man just as soon hop a train in Fulton, Kentucky, wind up in

Nashville, New Orleans, Texas, or San Francisco. Get off for a while, turn right around come right back. Always moving to keep busy. No work. Keep busy. Anything to keep busy. Just remember what the old men say, "This Hoover depression ain't gonna last forever."

One thing you've got to understand. Riding the rails can be deadly if you're not careful and know what you're doing. You want to catch the *front* of the car, and then if you happen to slip most likely you'll just be knocked backward away from the train. Great Uncle John Curtis Pate (son of Mary Elizabeth and Hillary) had a job as a brakeman on the railroad out of Fulton, Kentucky. One rainy night he got careless, swung on the boxcar from the rear, lost his grip, fell under the wheels and was crushed and cut all to pieces. There wasn't even enough left to scrape up for a decent burial.

A nother cold, wet night on the rails, another town somewhere in Missouri heading toward Cape. Chet's wearing thin khakis, tee shirt, tennis shoes without socks, but I'm better off wearing jeans, wool socks, plow shoes, and a sweater. We have one blanket to share, one canteen of water, and a few green apples left over from Anna, Illinois.

We're riding in a recently-used foul-smelling cattle car where we'll be standing for a while, slipping and swaying the rest of the way; or we'll pay the consequences.

When Chet and I took to the rails a few months ago, it was a different deal. The plan was to make some money picking apples in Anna, Illinois, cotton in Lake County, Tennessee, and on to Memphis for a job on a steamboat, working our way to New Orleans. At least that's the way it was supposed to be. After New Orleans? We had no plan. Just go on, I guess, like the river. Leave it alone and let it find its own sweet way.

If things work out, a little book could happen—we'll call it *A Vagabond Journey Through the South*. This idea came to me while reading Richard Halliburton's *Royal Road to Romance*. Chet likes the title

Hobo Country, but "no big deal," he says. "What difference it's gonna make anyway?"

So here we are: standing ankle deep in slick cow manure, dead tired and hungry, homesick, traveling west when I thought we were going east toward Kentucky or Tennessee closer to home. This is not a lonesome Jimmy Rogers blue yodel song I've heard Mom sing—*"All around the water tank, sleeping in the rain. I'm a thousand miles away from home just waiting for a train. . . ."* This is life the way it is.

I look at Chet in his filthy tee shirt shivering behind a grin, "Are we having fun yet?" he asks. It's hard to hear through the roar of the wind and the wheels whacking the tracks.

"Are we having fun?"

"Laugh all you want, mister know-it-all," I say, "but yes, we are. Someday, you wait and see, when we're famous and have all the money in the world, you're gonna remember this time as the happiest time in your life."

My prediction turned out to be right on the money—the happy part I mean. Pretty soon we started drifting apart and when the towns started filling up and running over with soldiers from Camp Tyson, Chet and I both could feel the hot draft breathing down our necks. Our last outing together turned out to be taking our dates to see *Pride of the Yankees* with Gary Cooper and Teresa Wright at the Capitol Theater in Paris, Tennessee. The newsreel was full of war.

We went our separate ways, March 10, 1943 to be exact. I volunteered for the marines and then the paratroops before I was drafted into the army from Detroit. Chet, determined to see the world, volunteered soon after for the navy. We promised to stay close as brothers, but didn't because there just wasn't enough time. There is never enough time to do all that needs to be done. Life keeps getting in the way.

For the rest of my life, especially in the dark of night, when I hear the lonesome wail of a freight train's whistle, I'll feel the hair standing up on my neck. The old feeling will flood over me. I'll remember my youth, innocence, adventure, and freedom, and I'll have the urge to hit the rails again, but I'm still working on my book. I don't know where it's taking me, but I'm still going.

Funny thing though—I still love rivers, railroads, and rabbit stew. I kid you not.

> Most of all I like the endless river,
> Stretched as far as I can see.
> I like the way moonlight plays on the water
> The way it moves.
> Always going somewhere.
> If I should ever die,
> Scatter my ashes from the big bridge
> And I'll be happy the rest of the way.

Last Furlough

I waited until the last day to tell my sweetheart goodbye.
The day was wet with showers but warm with a gentle
wind from the valley. We parked near the road at Red
Top hill and walked, holding hands, the quarter mile
or so through the woods to the rocky bluff overlooking
the valley, took shelter from the showers under heavy
old cedar trees—a private world walled by fog and mist.
She was laughing with tears and makeup streaking her
face. We didn't have to say goodbye. We just knew.

Mid-morning, April 10, 1944

PFC John Clubb, my buddy from the newly formed 22nd Hospital
Train, and I are packed and standing outside the main gate at Camp
Top Hat, Illinois, on the U. S. highway heading south, getting
ready to ride our thumbs home or as far as we can before catching
a Greyhound. John says, "Hitchhiking is as much mental as physical. Maybe more. Always give a big smile and wave, be positive and
confident."

It's an early spring morning, the kind you're likely to recall if
for no other reason than you feel lucky to be alive and you're going
home, home sweet home.

The man on the radio was right: Today we can expect overcast
skies and showers with temperatures dropping into the low 40s.
John and I have been standing on the road for an hour, grinning and
thumbing with no success, positive thinking is not working. As a
rule a GI uniform is a sure fire guarantee of a ride, sometimes with

a full meal and cigarettes to boot, but not today. Too many soldiers going home. Once in a while a car whizzes by. We wave. No one slows down. John's pacing in small circles, clapping his hands. "Man I dunno, think we oughta walk to town and see about a bus or train?" I'm about to agree when a dark blue '40 model Ford with white, sugar donut sidewalls and chrome spotlights slides up in a shower of gravel. We recognize the car and its driver, our own First Sergeant Matthew O'Doule.

"You boys wanna ride south?" The raspy tone is more command than invitation. Not waiting for an answer, O'Doule reaches across and opens the passenger side door. "Come on, that's the way I'm going. You're welcome to keep me company and spell me driving."

O'Doule looks sharp in a tailor-made dress uniform with burnished copper buttons, stripes running half-way up his arms, a high and tight GI haircut and a fresh shave, his face patched with little pieces of toilet paper. Reeking of after-shave lotion, he could almost pass for a regular GI on furlough.

John and I exchange glances as much to say this is really not what I had in mind. "John," I mutter out of the side of my mouth, "I'm not sure this is such a good idea. Whatcha think?" "I think you worry too much, Freeland. Follow me," John grins and slips into the front seat. "Oh, what the hell?" I get in the back, shove some stuff over, and settle down to get warm and comfortable.

The big Ford spins off.

"Fellas, there's some beer in the cooler back there. Help yourself and hand me another one." O'Doule turns on the radio, dials across local stations. Weather reports, farm news, static, preaching. Now from WLS Chicago, the pure sweet music of Duke Ellington's band, *Take the "A" Train*. Leave it there, I think, but say nothing. I think of telling Sgt. O'Doule and John that I saw the Duke once in Chicago and once in Detroit. I carried my date to see the Duke in a little for-blacks-only theater on Woodward Avenue. Also I saw his band at State and Lake Theater in Chicago. But I doubt they'd believe me.

Through the blue-haze of his cigar smoke, I can tell O'Doule's already pretty well lit up and feeling no pain. He wears a big absent-minded grin with his cap set at a rakish angle; beads of sweat collect on his forehead and upper lip.

O'Doule's hard to figure out. There's a side of O'Doule most people wouldn't know about, a side I discovered one night while I was doing extra duty cleaning his office. I rummaged through his desk looking for the week's KP list (or other intelligence that I might find helpful) and found a fist full of poems in his handwriting. This dragon writes poetry! I also found a copy of *Canterbury Tales*, *The Philosophy of William James*, and a dog-eared *King James Bible* signed with love from Momma.

O'Doule settles on clear channel 650 Nashville. "Okay, leave it there," I'm thinking. "Man, we can follow WSM all the way home. Home, sweet home."

Miles slip by under the hypnotic whomp whomp of the tires against asphalt. I'm feeling no pain. More bottles of Pabst Blue Ribbon beer make the rounds. Through the windows I smell the freshly plowed fields along the way. Every mile takes us closer home.

Home will feel like early summer: green trees, dogwoods, wild plums, redbuds in bloom. I'm starting to doze off when I hear O'Doule and John laughing. O'Doule says, "Hell, John call me Matt. We're just three ole boys on furlough. Going home," he looks over his shoulder. "Ain't that right, Freeland? Ain't that right?"

"You got that right, Sergeant."

O'Doule pulls over to the shoulder of the road, gets out, pulls off his uniform jacket heavy with chevrons and ribbons and hands it to John. "Here, Johnny, put this on. You're gonna be First Sergeant for a while."

"What?" John looks surprised.

"Put on the damn jacket."

"Uh, Top, I'd rather not do that."

"Do it. That's an order."

John shakes his head but puts on the jacket.

By the time we reach Carbondale, small fingers of late afternoon sun poke through red and purple clouds in the west promising a spell of good weather. . . . Red skies at night, sailor's delight. Red skies in the morning, sailor take warning.

"Well, men," O'Doule says, "Are you hungry? This is as good a place as any to stop and gas up. Ole Betsy here's running on empty and so am I."

O'Doule pulls in to a clean looking Gulf Station on the main drag near the railroad tracks, fills the gas tank, and adds a quart of oil.

We leave the car and walk across the street to a flashing na-ked-lady neon sign advertising Mom's Place. John's still wearing the sergeant stripes, O'Doule's in shirtsleeves. I'm bringing up the rear watching the pair. O'Doule's middle-aged, at least thirty-three to thirty-five years old, yet still moves well with the grace of an athlete. His downside is a small beer gut. John, my age nineteen, walks like a farmer, stiff-legged

In the old army, any soldier could challenge the First to a fist-fight and become first sergeant; and if you lost, it wouldn't be held against you. At least that's what they say. Thank God, this is not the old army. I'd hate to challenge this dude for sure. This is the new civilian army.

Mom's is Honky-Tonk, USA, the air thick with cigarette smoke, stale beer, the heavy odor of hot grease, burgers and onions. This could be Chief's Place, The Bloody Bucket, or any other joint back home, except for college girls jitterbugging with each other.

We find a dark corner booth, settle down, order cheeseburgers, double fries, onion rings, and three pitchers of draft beer. Sgt O'Doule (I'm still not entirely comfortable with this first name Matt business) swaggers over to the jukebox to punch up music and check out the babes.

John and I touch our beer mugs, "Chug-a-lug," I say. "How's this? On furlough with the top dragon and money to spend . . . eat your heart out."

"I got no complaints."

The beer is frosty cold and plenty of it. "Yeah," John says, "only one more thing could make it perfect and she's standing over there by the jukebox."

I look and catch my breath. There's an angel wearing a tight pink sweater, plaid skirt, brown and white saddle shoes. Angel face flips her shoulder length blond hair and looks over at us. I think of the song, *Sweet and Lovely* from the June Allison movie, *Two Girls and a Sailor*. All at once it hits me. I'm lonesome and homesick. I want to go home and never leave again, and I want to take sweet and lovely June Allison with me and never go to war. I know in my deepest heart, I'm in love with June Allison. I must have said it out loud, "I'm in love with June Allison."

"What? What are you talking about?" John says

"I said, I'm in love with that babe over there looking at us. Either you make a move or I'm sure going to."

"Help yourself if you think you're big enough. It's a free country."

"John, we've been in the field too damn long, *all* the babes look good.

"You know . . . someday Freeland, we'll have chicks in *our* army. I've heard the Russians do. If that ever happens, I'm a twenty-year man."

"Dream on, fool, but you do have a point. The thing wrong with this man's army, it's an all man's army. I want to smell some perfume. Feel something soft, for Pete's sake."

"I hear you loud and clear, shut up and drink your beer. Hey! That rhymes. I'm a poet and don't know it." John reaches for the pitcher and pours himself another beer and grins at it.

From the jukebox comes Harry James, *I Know I've Heard that Song Before.* I think of double-timing Margaret and the movie, "Springtime in the Rockies" with Harry James. The last time we were together we saw that movie. I wonder who she's seeing now. I know she's not sitting home alone, that's for sure. I don't care.

I can't remember girls' names so well but I do remember the music, where we were on a date . . . *Stardust* on the radio, *Sunrise Serenade, Moonlight Serenade.* Know what I mean?

"John, our beer is running low."

John says, "There's more where that came from. We're on furlough. Got money in our pockets. Let 'er roll."

John looks—I think the word is *resplendent*—in 1st Sgt's jacket, even two sizes too big.

"Johnny, Harry James is one lucky dog."

"What brought that up?"

"Well, hell, he's married to Betty Grable, ain't he?"

"Drink up. Your beer's getting hot."

"She must have married him for his music. He's one ugly dude."

Yeah, well, how about Sgt. O'Doule. Same thing, right?"

"I don't follow you."

"My point is, O'Doule's ugly as sin yet all the women are nuts about him. Ain't that so?"

"That don't prove a damn thing, Freeland. God himself couldn't understand a woman and I sure don't pretend to. They're hard to live with and they're hard to live without. OK, try this: women like strong ugly men. Right? Women love convertibles and money and power. Put all that together it spells Matthew O'Doule. Bingo." John is leaning on the table doodling dollar signs and hearts, dollar signs and hearts. I think I could track John all across America just following his little doodles.

"Yes," I say, "ole Matt does okay with women."

"He's a funny guy, not bad when you get to know him."

"Speak of the devil," I say, "look yonder."

O'Doule's backed into a corner by two big bruisers. One holds a knife, the other a beer bottle by the neck. Except for Harry James on the jukebox, the room has become hushed. Quiet. O'Doule looks cool, relaxed, smiling.

Suddenly I feel flushed hot, but cold at the same time and can't move.

I remember what happened next as a dream. Parts in slow motion like when you don't know whether you're dreaming or half awake.

O'Doule's sudden scream. O'Doule's a blur spinning, kicking, head-butting, fist punching (not swinging but straight to the target pistons.) The knife comes slithering across the floor landing at the bartender's feet. In maybe five seconds, one trucker's on the floor, the other huddled under a table.

Harry James hasn't missed a beat.

Things could have gone from bad to worse in a hurry if the bartender had called the cops. We could have spent our last furlough in the Carbondale jail facing court martial. Not smart.

The bartender actually saves our skins. Instead of reaching for the telephone, he reaches behind the bar for a large ugly double-barreled shotgun, "Gentlemen," he says in a quiet voice, "may I please have your attention?" With that shotgun in hand, he immediately has what he requests. Glancing from O'Doule to the truckers and finally fixing his gaze on John and me, "Gentlemen, we run a nice little establishment here. Our little home you, might say. A family place where men and women of all faiths can come together for libation and companionship." He moves closer to our table holding the big well-oiled cannon cradled in his arm, pointing to O'Doule and staring John straight in the eyes, "Sergeant, I'm giving you exactly twenty-eight seconds to get that crazy private out of here."

[19]

We double-time back to the car, laughing like idiots, and burn rubber toward Kentucky singing a Jimmy Rogers blue yodel song.

> *Oh, they put me off in Texas,*
> *A state I dearly love,*
> *Wide open spaces all round me*
> *The moon and stars above . . .*

O'Doule lets me out in Paducah where I'll have no trouble catching a ride south to Henry County. John and Matt head on east toward Hopkinsville.

Paducah is much smaller than I remember. Two summers ago when I caught a bus from here to Chicago, it was a good-sized city. Now I'm amazed how much it's shrunk. Neon lights still blink on Broadway, but without the glitter and wonder. The shops are not as rich; the sidewalks are not as wide; even Hotel Irvin Cobb is less splendid.

I walk on toward the river and the train station. There should be a bench where I can sack out for the night. Right now I'm tired and a little hungover from too much O'Doule and beer, but still too hyped up to think about sleeping. Soon I'll be home for ten whole days before saying goodbye again. Saying goodbye is the hardest part of leaving.

Home

Today I'm home
Among ancient moss-covered
Rocks: my friends.
Fractured rays of first sun
Poke through leafy branches
Over my head.
I drink cold water
From the stream
With darting minnows.
Frogs and snakes.
The water is fresh
With ferns and healing magic.
This is my place
Alone
Listening to the music
Of rushing water
And the lonesome call
Of whippoorwills.

The season could have been any season bees fly; the year could have been any one after World War II. It really doesn't matter because like evening shadows, they're all soon gone yet timeless in one captured moment.

I've guessed right again. Dad is home sitting in the peach orchard watching his bees work. I do a double take, surprised at how much Dad resembles his father, still slim but bent over, direct piercing eyes, even the worn black felt hat sitting square on his head could have been my grandfather's.

He looks up, waves, motions for me to come near. "My bees are getting ready to swarm," he says. "Come sit down, be quiet and listen."

I've been through this drill before.

Above the sound of the bees I hear doves, chattering bobwhites, and somewhere on the hill a hammerhead woodpecker is hard at work.

The spring thaw has warmed the ground; the day is washed clean and bright from last night's showers. I scoop up a small handful of soil and smell rain, sunshine, decayed musky peach tree leaves all mixed together. The woods have turned from shades of gray and brown to radiant green.

This is home where time meanders at its own sweet pace, the sun comes up, the sun goes down, seasons change, and shadows fall. Over the years when my life gets screwed up, out of balance and too heavy to carry, I come here to remember who I am, call time out, breathe, cling close to nature, and renew myself. More important I'm free to be myself, I don't have to impress a living soul.

Above all I want to visit Dad for a while. I really do, though it's hard to admit and I'd sure never let him know.

Dad stands, motions "Come with me," and walks toward his shop. "I want to show you some hives I'm making."

We walk inside the shop. The floor is soft with sawdust—the air sharp with the smell of fresh cut pine lumber and paint.

Dad shows me his new beehives. "They're just as good as factory-made," he says. Carefully he gathers pine shavings and starts building a fire in the Franklin stove to chase the damp chill, then fiddles with his long stemmed pipe, crumbles home-cured tobacco into it, carefully tamps in the tobacco, and strikes a match with his thumb nail. I know what's coming next. "Son, the simple life is the best life. All a man needs to be happy is a good woman, few acres of land as far back off the road as he can get, a few hives of bees, a good garden, some fruit trees, grapevines, and a dog."

My dad, Mason Noel Freeland, the beekeeper, 1973.

I know his sermon like a song but I listen and take notes in my journal more from habit than anything else. "Live close to nature. A person needs clean air and quiet and peace—a place where you hear owls and whippoorwills at night." Dad smiles, "I'd recommend a bulldog and if somebody comes to bother me, somebody from the government, I'd sic the bulldog on him to tear the seat out of his britches."

My mind begins to wander. I'm eight again, the summer of 1932, my first day selling honey door to door. I'd take one side of the street with my five-pound pail of honey working door to door. Dad worked the other side carrying a pail in each hand. I doubled my sales when I grew older and strong enough to carry two buckets at the same time. My commission was twenty-five cents per sale, and on a good day, I would make anywhere from $2 to $2.50. At a time during the great depression and the dust bowl days when families, even those who lived on farms, often went hungry. Full grown men were glad to work on the state roads shoveling gravel or whatever other jobs they could find for a dollar a day, most times even less. Whenever a man would fall out from the heat, another man was always standing by ready to pick up his shovel and take his place.

I remember Dad's instructions "Stand up straight, pull your shoulders back. Remember, knock on the door. When a woman opens it, you take a step backwards, smile, take off your cap and ask, 'are you the lady of the house?' Most always she'll say yes. Then you say, 'Mam, I have some pure wild bee honey I want you to sample.' Look straight into her eyes, hand her the bucket of honey. She'll reach for it. If she should hesitate, say again, 'This is *pure wild bee honey* gathered from *wild flowers* and made in our own bee yard; just take it to the kitchen and sample it.' In a minute or so she'll come back without the honey. 'How much?' she'll ask. '*Only* a dollar,' you'll say.

"Now remember: say as little as possible. Make eye contact. Smile. Stand straight and still. When you do speak, speak up. Sometimes she'll ask questions like 'Where was this honey made, or what's it from?' *Always* tell the truth. This honey *is* from *wild* flowers. It *is* pure. It *is* good and good for you. Tell her we eat it every day on hot biscuits with butter. Son, that's a *personal endorsement* the best kind. If we didn't believe in our product, we wouldn't be selling it—same with any job. Do what you love . . . and the rest comes easy."

I look at Dad through a veil of his pipe smoke—a private man I hardly know, almost a stranger—and wonder at what point in time did I even begin to appreciate his talents—his genius in many ways? And why do I keep coming here to his workshop to listen to his stories, to argue and most of all, try to figure him out.

I pull a yard chair close to the stove and settle down, aware of the popping sound and the smell of the burning pine knots, fresh paint, pipe smoke and sawdust. This moment is bathed in the shadows of yesterday, like all the other days, all the other times, the years all the same—yet different.

Tacked on the far wall are family pictures, Tennessee and Kentucky maps, on a shelf the old brownish-red fiddle. There are also some books, a brown water jug, a bee smoker. And in the corner are gardening tools, a double-bit axe, and a weather-beaten wheat cradle. Every item and tool from bee smoker to the brown-clay water jug has a story to tell. I'm surprised to see the fiddle here of all places, cast aside like an old soldier when the war is over. I look at the fiddle and hear Dad or Pap sawing out square dance tunes. My mind floods with memories of box suppers and dances. I smile remembering Pap's joke, "Without this fiddle son there'd be no you." I never tired of any of his stories—especially of how he met Grandmother Ada. I know the story by heart: Pap—Johnny the fiddle player age 30 falling in love with 17 year old Ada Sally Ray one frosty Thanksgiving night at a fund raiser at the Blood River School.

"She never would have noticed me," my grandfather said, "except I was on the stage in the lantern light, playing the fiddle, cutting up, making a fool of myself. I thought she was the prettiest girl I'd ever seen, long black hair, dark brown eyes, shy smile. When I was fiddling a hoedown, I could see she wanted to dance. When I fiddled a slow sad song like *Barbra Allen* or *The Last Waltz with You*, I'd see her dark eyes fixed on me. I couldn't wait for the auction to start and I knew if I possibly could, I'd buy her box supper and get to eat with her.

"When it was time to start the bidding, the auctioneer knew exactly what was going on. He had that pretty girl come and stand beside him on the stage. He waited a few moments for silence. Someone called her name, 'Ada Ray, what's for supper?' I thought never you mind, I'm the one having supper with this pretty thing.

"The auctioneer started off high. 'Who'll bid one dollar for dinner with this pretty young lady?' My mouth was so dry I couldn't speak so I pulled off my hat and waved it. The bidding kept going. I keep waving until it's down to a couple of Clayton boys, Ollie Emerson, and me. The crowd's really enjoying the show. The bidding hit $4.50. It's Ollie and me and I can tell from Ollie's face, he's done. I'd have sold my horse and saddle if I'd had to.

"We joined the others after supper bobbing for apples and playing drop the handkerchief and hurry John. 'Ada Ray,' I said, 'This night is made especially for you. Look at that full harvest moon.' Between the dances when we stopped to rest, I put my coat around her shoulders to protect her from the chill of the evening. I thought my heart would bust.

"The very next spring (June 6, 1887) we were married at her family's home in Conyersville. It was the fiddle, son, two people met and fell in love because of a fiddle," he smiled and winked—"my salesmanship . . . and I expect you know the rest."

My grandfather, John Wesley Freeland, was my hero and one of the last pioneers. A small framed, hard muscled man, who brought his 17-year-old bride into an unsettled land, hacked out a living making crossties for the railroad at twenty-five cents apiece, and raising corn, hogs and tobacco. They say he could work all day behind a plow then fiddle half the night away for a square dance.

Truth is stranger than fiction. Mom and Dad met much the same way at musicals and box suppers in Weakley County near Gleason. Some of my first memories are watching Dad play while I hold onto Mom to keep her from dancing.

The fiddle passed into Dad's hands when Pap's fingers become too stiff and deformed to play. Dad soon played square dance tunes

Soldier's Joy, Turkey in the Straw, Saturday Night Waltz as well as anybody. He played with Holmes Jennings, Chester Yarbrough, and Rafe Freeland, some of the best fiddlers around. People said he played *Listen to the Mocking Bird* better than anybody else they'd ever heard. You could just about see the pretty bird sitting on a limb singing.

In the late summer of 1928 when I was just past four, the fiddle carried us all the way to Arkansas west of Hot Springs, not too far from the Texas state line. "Not in a million years," Dad said, "not in my wildest dreams had I ever thought about going west. Except for Zane Grey books I knew nothing."

Early summer the heavy slow season before fall, Dad was in the bottom field laying-by the last rows of corn. He looked up and saw Jim Wilson, a close neighbor approaching. Wonder what the old man wants coming way down here, Dad thought. Mr. Wilson walked closer and waved, "Mason, I've been looking for you. I'm here to ask a favor."

"Mr. Jim, tell me what I can do for you."

"Well, you may want to think some first. Me and Alice are getting on. We want you to move us to Arkansas so we can be with our son and his family. If you're up to doing it, we'll pay you what's fair."

"Arkansas's an awful long way, Mr. Jim," Dad paused, "and I'm not sure my old car would make it, but tell you what. Let me think about it and talk to Wilby some and I'll let you know."

A day or so later Mr. Wilson came to the house, "My boy says he'll get a musical and a square dance together for you and Wilby can sing if you'll come out. He says you all can make a good living out there playing your music."

Dad didn't hesitate. "I'll start getting the car ready." Mom and Dad worked late into the night packing and looking at maps. I woke several times and they were still working and talking.

Next morning, a Tuesday, Mom and Dad helped the Wilsons load everything they owned into the back seat of our topless 1915 T model Ford. Heavy stuff for balance on the bottom, a spare wheel and tire, quilts, a wash pot filled with family pictures and keepsakes, straw ticking mattress, fruit jars and jugs, garden tools they couldn't bear to leave behind, a shot gun, and at the top of the pyramid, two feather beds, rain gear, tarpaulin, a wicker basket of food, jars of water, and Mrs. Wilson's Bible. The Wilsons watched over all their goods from the very top of the pyramid perched on a feather bed and quilts

My place was up front with Mom and Dad, hard against Mom's guitar, Dad's fiddle, the 22-caliber Stevens rifle, and our change of clothing.

The empty smooth-graded gravel road led west through fields of cotton and corn, pastures with cattle, silos and cotton gins. Once in a while we passed through a small town, crossed rivers on temporary bridges or ferries on westward toward Memphis, across the Mississippi then Arkansas—toward wonder and mystery.

Dad drove every mile with only brief rest stops for gas and oil, water in the radiator, and cold coca colas.

"These are the friendliest people I've ever seen in my life," Dad said. "They come running, laughing and waving all the time."

"I guess that's the way people out here act," Mr. Wilson said.

Miss Alice has perked up and is enjoying herself, "They must think we're a traveling show. Maybe they think we're part of a carnival."

At a Gulf station in Brownsville from his perch high atop all his goods, Mr. Wilson hollered to a man in a suit and polished shoes, "Hey Boy, come over here." The man turned, looked surprised, and came to the car. "Here, Boy, take this dollar to the store and buy me a cap. My head's getting burned." The man took the dollar went into a dry-goods store and came back carrying a cap.

"Let's move on, Mason," Mom said in a tired voice. "We can make it to Memphis before dark."

Memphis is a lot farther than any of us could imagine. A place none of us has ever seen before, sitting beside the muddy Mississippi where people sing songs about riverboats, hobos, women, and lonely trains passing in the night. But Memphis is a dangerous place. It's the biggest city in the world.

In the gathering dark, tall buildings stand outlined against the red sky. I can't swallow my excitement.

From above our heads, "Lordy. Lordy. Praise Jesus."

For the rest of her life, Mom talked about the trip, "Mason and I were so young. Only 24. We'd never been anywhere. I've never been so tired in my life and so scared. One night west of Memphis, Mason was worn out from driving and sleepy. He told me 'I've just got to stop for a few winks or I'm gonna run off the road.' It must have been sometime after midnight. The blackest night I've ever seen. We hadn't seen another car for hours. Mason fell sound asleep; so were the others. At first the woods around us were quiet and still. Not a sound except the car's radiator popping as it cooled off. Then just as I was starting to drift off, the night slowly started to come alive with all kinds of strange sounds. Frogs, peepers, whippoorwills, owls. One owl would call, another would answer. But then something close by squalls out sounding like a woman or a child. I guess it was a cougar. Whatever it was I've never been so scared in my life: I shook Mason awake and told him we've got to move on! I often think what if that old car wouldn't have started."

Another long day on the road. Flat country with small farms and ranches turn into thick forest-covered hills and mountains. Late afternoon we top a long rise and slowly roll into a valley. Mom points to the map, smiles, "This is Hot Springs!" Her hand is shaking.

"Hot Springs National Park, Arkansas," Dad echoes.

Clouds of steam come from springs and streams.

"Lordy, lordy, burning springs," Miss Alice says. "Never in my life did I ever expect to see anything like this. No telling what else we'll find."

"Well," Dad said, "Let's stretch our legs and fill up, then we'll drive on. Sure hope we have a good turnout for the dance . . . that's what I'm thinking about."

Dance All Night
with a Bottle in Your Hand

People start showing up at the Wison house by late afternoon for the jamboree. They gather on the front porch and in the big front room now clear of all furniture except for a few cane bottom chairs. Others stand outside under the trees talking and impatiently waiting to dance or listen to the music. Some gather in small groups, visiting with neighbors and family they haven't seen in a while.

Mom is in the front room speaking to people, but Dad stands outside the door and waits until the last minute to enter the room. He wears new Levis, starched blue work shirt and polished brown plow shoes, a fresh shave with his black hair slicked back.

People say Dad could pull a crowd playing a washboard or beating a tub—a natural showman, promoter, and a salesman. They say Mom's the artist, the quiet one content and happy to let him be the star.

Dad holds up the fiddle reflecting light from the lanterns, his fingers coiled around its neck, thumping catgut strings. The showman's already at work doing his thing, making the audience wait, enjoying every minute of it.

The fiddler starts off slow setting the mood—pure emotion: *Cowboy's Lament* followed by *The Saturday Night Waltz*. A few young couples join hands, start round dancing. More dancers move to the floor.

My parents, Mason Noel Freeland and
Wilby Lee Murphy Freeland, wedding picture, 1923.

A harmony number is next, *In the Valley:*

> *Down in the valley*
> *Valley so low*
> *Hang your head over*
> *Hear the wind blow*

Another popular valley song *Red River Valley:*

> *Oh, from this valley they say you are going*
> *Do not hasten to bid me adieu*
> *Just remember the Red River Valley*
> *And the girl who loves you so true.*

Now the fiddler ups the tempo with *Soldier's Joy* and follows that with *Turkey in the Straw*. The dancers get down to business.

After the break it's Mom's turn. No showmanship needed. No pretense. Just sweet pure from the heart Wilby Lee. She started with *Knoxville Girl*, a story from the old country set to music about a young girl from Knoxville town whose jealous lover killed her down by the river. All the while she's pleading and saying, Sweetheart I love you so. People stopped dancing and gathered around listening. "Wilby Lee ought to be on XERA!"

She sang Jimmy Rogers hobo songs:

> *All around the water tank*
> *Sleeping in the rain,*
> *I'm a thousand miles away from home*
> *Just waiting for a train.*

This one brought the house down. Lemon said, "I could hear that lonely train whistling and just about feel the rain and wind in my face."

The pretty black haired woman spun a magic of her own: honest magic, pure feeling emotion to stab the heart. She sang *Wildwood Flower* with tears in her eyes.

> *Oh he taught me to love him and promised to love*
> *And to cherish me over all others above*
> *How my heart is now wondering no misery can tell*
> *He's left me no warning, no words of farewell.*

Finally almost midnight near the end Mom danced the Charleston, the new dance craze sweeping the county.

"Well, Mason," Lemon Wilson said, "They sure got their money's worth that's for sure. We can do a musical every month with an ice cream supper thrown in between and make money. I heard them talking. They like you both and I heard them say Wilby Lee sings better than Maybelle Carter. You folks go on back and get your things. I'll talk up a jamboree for next month."

Mom and Dad never went back to Arkansas. Several times I've asked them, "Why not? You liked the country a lot and you liked the people, right? The people there sure welcomed you and your music." I think it could have been the depression. They were both afraid to pull up stakes and go off to start over. Dad liked to say, "We've got a little toe holt here and a little piece of land paid for, we'd better stick it out here."

They continued to play from time to time at county school musicals and 4th of July at Sulfur Well, but little more. Then the family started growing when my brother Randy was born in 1930. By the time Jim came along in 1939, they'd stopped playing altogether except practicing at home once in a while.

Amazing Grace

More than twenty years have quietly slipped away,
without so much as a whisper since Dad died. Of
my trips to inventory and collect my books, papers,
and anything else left of value, one trip stands out
above all the others. The old shop waited for me in
damp darkness. I was surprised at its stillness, the
absolute quiet, the nothingness. As I waited for a few
moments for my eyes to adjust, I smelled pipe smoke,
fresh cut pine lumber and the aroma of burning pine
knots. Momentarily I felt that I was not alone. I
felt the presence of the Bee Man as real as today.

The boxes and trunks are covered with spider webs, dust, and
dirt dauber nests. I reached under a stack of old newspapers
and magazines and pulled out a chicken snake as big as my arm. A
harmless snake but it could just as well have been a cottonmouth or
copperhead. Mom's guardian angel is still looking over my shoulder.

So many old pictures, letters, stuff now too precious to throw
away. Every item sparks a memory. A rusty tobacco knife and I'm
back in the tobacco patch doing the hardest, most backbreaking
work I've ever done. And yesterday under some trash I found my
paratrooper boots, spit-shine turned to mold, cracked from age, half
eaten by rats and mice. I kept looking and found my World War II
Eisenhower jacket hanging in the smokehouse holding a family of
flying squirrels and wren's nest.

The faded letter postmarked Berlin, 1949, still waits for answer—how long? How many years? Seven lines, seventy-nine words. *Do you remember me?*

Dear Friend, do you remember me? I often think of you
And wonder how you are in America.
I often think of our time. It seems such a long time ago yet
such a short time—five years. I'm now 21, your age when we met.
    Life is hard here. We are cut off and surrounded by the Russians. I don't like asking but I must tell you that I am hungry. Please help if you can. Lilli

I don't think I ever knew her last name or if I did I've forgotten it. I remember teasing her . . . "You are the girl in the song Lilli Marlene."

In the poem/song from the First World War, the young fraulein waits at the gate for her soldier. Lilli and I met much the same way.

I was standing first guard at the barracks gate one foggy night when Lilli and her older sister riding bikes stopped to talk. The next night she came back alone.

The Lilli I knew has become as lost in myth and mystery as the Lilli Marlene in the song—the story of a girl left behind waiting wistfully under the lantern for her soldier to return.

In 1969, at a Jesse Stuart creative writer's workshop, I tried to recapture the beautiful sad-eyed girl in the short story "Return to Green River."

I wrote of short days of summer turning into the colors of early fall, of bike rides into the countryside to escape the city. I wrote of one early morning when our company loaded up and left for home.

We said goodbye at the guard's gate where we met. We laughed and made small talk until it was time to go. I remember the chilly early fall day with the smell of wood smoke and frost in the air.

I slung my bags over my shoulder and started walking to the bus. She ran after me. "*Bitte, bitte, nich forgissen meir,*" she said. (Please, please don't forget me.)

Now for a moment or so in the shadows and fragments of my past, I stand again at the guard's gate near the barracks in war-torn Berlin and wait.

In a brown manila envelope I found a few of our son Steve's poems mixed with some school papers and books. On one poem, the *Beekeeper,* Ellen had written, "Steve died 10 years and 6 months to the day after Daddy died. Mom Freeland had been dead almost nineteen years. Her death in March 1960 was the first in our family."

Steve wrote of his experiences in Coventry where he spent the summer after his graduation from the University of the South in Sewanee, Tennessee.

Coventry Cathedral
July 2, 1976

Dear Family,
We are scorching in the heat. Temperatures in Coventry are in the 90's and we have not had any rain for weeks so this is a hot, dry summer—the hottest ever in England. It is, in fact, a drought so devastating that the water supply of the mid and south east portions of England will be exhausted within 37 days and unless we have rain we will be forced onto water rations.

In the back of Kennedy House we have a small garden we are battling to save. Thus far it is in good condition but if we go onto water rations here I believe that the garden will probably dehydrate.

I have some interesting things to say about this garden; that it was once worked by the Benedictine monks in the 12th century when they had a monastery in the area on which the new cathedral now stands. After the dissolution of the monasteries the ground was left unworked for centuries so that the soil regenerated and has become very rich. But during the construction of the St. Michael's Parish church, and later, the area of the garden was used for dumping wastes such as old tiles and stone and rocks. Today in order that we get back to the rich subsoil we must sift through several feet of rock (literally sift—throwing shovels of rock against a large wire mesh screen to salvage what dirt we can from the rock).

This is how I spent my day yesterday and I plan to spend several hours of my free time doing work of this sort in the garden. Yet, in answer to Mom's question, I say that my most substantial work is as a guide in the cathedral. Although I also work in the International Center and the Centre for Studies. Also, as I am the only Student of our group who is on a full scholarship from the Cathedral, I have been made the Senior member and represent our group at the weekly staff meetings.

I spent last Sunday at the home of the Woof family. We had brunch then Mr. Woof and I took a walk about the district and into the country. I was astonished to learn that even in the rural areas of England, the government must force residents into as dense an area as can be made so that farm lands which are scarce on this island might be reserved. England imports 50% of their food.

The English romanticize notions of space. In speaking

with people, I have learned that of those who wish to come to the U.S.A. they each say, without exception, that they wish to see the Grand Canyon—our emblem of space,

Love,

Stephen

P. S. during my visit with the Woof family, we attended an Evensong service in a small parish church which is over 700 years old.

I carefully read the letter again. I don't believe in reincarnation, but if I did, this letter could have been written by my grandfather, John Wesley Freeland. Steve's words and between the lines echo a deep respect for the land, just as Pap loved the land and lived his life.

It's all there: the love and respect of the land and of nature. The dignity of hard work and service to others. I see also his unending search for the mystery called God.

Digging deeper among the magazines and school papers, pictures and letters, a Fayetteville, Tennessee, postmark catches my eye

Dear Mom and family,

I'll be taking the job at Fayetteville's new station (Fayetteville is 70 miles south of Nashville and 17 miles north of Huntsville, Alabama). This is my kind of town with a majestic courthouse, and colonial homes on tree lined streets that remind me of the movie, Gone With the Wind.

I've made a friend with a pretty girl just out of high school (robbing the cradle, right?) She's been working this summer at Standard Drugs and getting ready for college with a scholarship but I'm pretty sure she'll be working as a receptionist/bookkeeper at the station for a while. Her name is Flora Ellen

Yesterday we walked to the Elk River that runs through

High school graduation picture,
Flora Ellen Elmore, age 18,
Blanche High School, 1948.

town. She pointed out the historical marker where General
Andrew Jackson and his troops camped on the way to New
Orleans. I'll send pictures as soon as they're developed.

You can send my mail to the Largen Hotel. I'll be staying
there until I can find a more permanent room that I can afford.

With all my love and appreciation for everything you mean
to me.

Mike

Radio Romance

I have in mind a plan of development
which would make radio a household
utility in the same sense as the piano
or phonograph. The idea is to bring
music into the house by wireless.

—David Sarnoff, in a 1915
memorandum to Edward J. Nully,
Marconi Wireless Telegraph Company

October 2, 1948
Largen Hotel, Fayetteville, Tennessee

A cool breeze with a hint of coming winter fans the curtains in my
room. The wind, the smells and sound of my favorite season only
add to my feeling of emptiness. On days like this I wonder where I
am. Who am I? And too often, why am I? I'm alone in a hotel in a
strange town. Surely if I had the brains of a frog I'd be back in the
army and with a little luck I'd be in Europe in school with Uncle
Sam's GI bill picking up the tab.

Misery loves company. I'm slowly rereading Thomas Wolfe's *Of
Time and the River*, this time with my pencil in hand underlining
and making notes. Here Wolfe describes a scene from a train that's
so descriptive of war:

It is a place that is savage and cruel, but it is also the innocent place; it is the wild and lawless place, the vital earth

that is soaked with the blood of the murdered men . . . it is also the place of the child and laughter where the young men are torn apart with ecstasy and cry out in their throats with joy, where they hear the howl of the wind and the rain and smell the thunder and the soft numb spitting of the snow, where they are drunk with the bite and sparkle of the air and mad with the solar energy, where they believe in love and victory and think that they can never die.

I think of my silent past—the winter of 1944-45 in the cold snowbound Ardennes forest, that same earth soaked with the blood of the murdered men (for that is what war is, legal murder). I think of the silent ones left behind. The brave ones left in unmarked graves or under the white crosses.

My bad days in the deepest holes of my mind leave me angry, full of conflict and frustration. On bad days I'd like most of all to be able to throw up my hands and just disappear. Most of all from myself.

The nights are worst of all. Long, never ending, when sleep won't come. I seem to have this heavy weight hanging over me, surrounding me like a black cloud and I remember every bad thing I've ever done in my life. I try reading or writing, walking. Many times I've walked away half the night with my mind somewhere else when I suddenly realize I'm lost. I console myself knowing I can get through one day at a time—one hour at a time, if I must. All the while dreading the thought of tomorrow.

The bad times will pass. The sun will break through the black clouds and for no reason at all, I'm on a mountain again. There's hardly ever any in-between.

Now I watch the light filter through the curtains and wait and listen for the town to come alive. Today the sky will be blue with little gray puffs of clouds, and like most fall days, the smell of burning leaves in the air. I wait for another day to unravel. Down the street a hundred yards or so Mars Café will be serving breakfast. Twenty-two cents will buy me two scrambled eggs, bacon, grits, toast and coffee.

Life is good again.

People having breakfast at Mars Café are buzzing about the opening of the radio station. It's been the talk of the town for weeks. Some wondered if it would really happen. Gordon Turner from *The Nashville Tennessean* stopped in for coffee. He'll write all about the opening.

His story appeared in Monday's paper.

The newest enterprise in this town, radio station WEKR started off with a bang Friday in a dedicatory breakfast program at the pretty Fayetteville Country Club, attended by 200 business and professional men of Middle Tennessee.

Owned and operated by R. A. Largen and associates, the 250-watt station located in all-new quarters at the edge of town on the Pulaski highway, went on the air at 6 a.m. The elaborate christening ceremonies began at 8 a.m. when guests assembled for breakfast in the beautifully arranged dining room of the country club just north of town. The Mother's Club headed by Mrs. Charles Parks served coffee, fruit juices, and an assortment of sweet cakes on flower-strewn tables while a log fire in the big open fireplace took the chill out of the crisp fall morning.

Program director Frank Huber introduced A. D. Smith Jr., general manager of both the Winchester radio station and WEKR here, who extended thanks to all who had helped to bring radio to Fayetteville. He introduced the 30-odd guests of honor from Franklin, Shelbyville, Pulaski, Tullahoma, Nashville, Chattanooga, Lynchburg and Winchester.

Welcoming the new business to the city here was D. T. Buchanan, mayor for 14 years and long-time local NC&St.L

railway agent. Ed H. Morgan, manager of the station, introduced the eight staff members, some of whom, he said, had come to make Fayetteville their new home.

R. A. ("Andy") Largen who is largely responsible for WEKR's birth here declared his sole interest was to help his town and county have everything all other good towns have. "This is your public service agent," he said. "We want all our citizens to use and enjoy it and make suggestions for making it of most value to us. May it go forth today to serve, and God bless us all."

Sarnoff's music box came alive in 1920 when KDKA in Pittsburgh and WWJ in Detroit started broadcasting. Soon other stations followed and throughout America, for the first time all across the country, in crossroads villages, small towns and cities, lonely farm houses, and other places, enchanted listeners surrounded their radio receivers—or those of their neighbors—and were captured in a common community that was radio.

My family's first radio was a battery powered Philco—a beautiful thing sitting on a table near the window. Its thin wire antenna ran under the window and on to the top of the tallest oak tree at the creek bank.

Radio became my companion, teacher, and my first guide to lead me away to a larger world.

I went south to New Orleans and to Mexico (thanks to clear channel XERA). I watched the St. Louis Browns and Cardinal baseball games on KMOX.

Family and neighbors gathered almost every Saturday night for front row seats to the Grand Ole Opry at the Ryman Auditorium in Nashville—reserved seats courtesy of WSM and our Philco.

June 22, 1937, Comiskey Park, Chicago, I saw the heavyweight championship fight between James J. Braddock and challenger Joe

October 2, 1948, Open House for the new radio station. The WEKR staff pictured in the new studio: Seated in front, Melba Chick, traffic and Ellen Elmore, bookkeeper/receptionist. Standing left to right: Mike Freeland, news director; Frank Huber, program director; Ed Morgan, station manager; Elton Chick, chief engineer; Ernest Tucker, engineer; and Art Smith, general manager.

Louis. A sellout—even with general admission tickets costing $3.75, ringside $27.50, but I had the best seat in the house at ringside free—at Aunt Zella's house on her new battery powered radio. I'm crowded within a tight circle: Dad and Mom, Harris, Aunt Zella, my cousin Ruby Doris, up close in the pale blue light of the radio's dial.

The announcer: *"Ladies and Gentlemen!"* Swelling waves of applause break the night. I'm shivering with excitement. *"In this corner wearing purple trunks weighing one hundred ninety-seven and a quarter pounds, the challenger from Detroit, Michigan, Joe Louis!"* Again the crowd goes crazy. Louis dances to the center of the ring, waves to the crowd, his black skin glistening under the lights.

"And in this corner wearing white trunks, weighing 197 pounds from

Pittsburgh, Pennsylvania, the undisputed heavyweight champion of the world . . . James J. Braddock!"

Again the crowd goes wild. Braddock is the crowd favorite. He tosses aside his green robe and moves to the center of the ring, arms upraised. The two fighters stand together listening to the referee's instructions.

I can't wait.

My heart is thumping. I smell the strong odor of rubbing alcohol, the thick rich fumes of cigar smoke and sweat. It's a hot night but I'm chilled.

The fighters touch gloves and go back to their corners. The bell rings.

Round one. *Braddock charges from his corner after Louis. Louis dances away, flicking left jabs, then a hard left by Louis. Braddock counters with his own left and a right cross blocked by Louis. Louis has Braddock in a corner. He's taking it to the champ. They're at close range exchanging punches. Louis is down! A short upper cut, but he bounces right up. Braddock after Louis. But Louis staggers Braddock with a left hook and a right cross at the bell.*

End of round one. Give it to Braddock.

The fight moves on round after round. Now it's the eighth round.

Louis is clearly in charge now. Braddock's game. Braddock's tired, hanging on. His legs are gone. He can't keep up. Braddock's eyes are puffed. There's a cut over the left side of his forehead streaming blood. Still he won't go down. Now here's the Brown Bomber moving in, measuring Braddock with the left. It's Louis with a left to the body—a right to the chin. Braddock's hurt! He's down!

Louis goes back to his corner.

Referee Tommy Thomas slowly counts to ten.

The fight is over. One minute ten seconds into the eighth round.

And I saw it all ringside on a small battery powered box spitting words through the air forming perfect pictures in my mind.

Most afternoons at five o'clock the WSM announcer switched

his microphone to the railroad tracks near the edge of town so that I could ride the fast flying Pan American Flyer . . . From a great distance I could hear the throbbing sound of the fast moving train—drawing closer—its warning whistle—now closer, another warning blast before thundering through our living room, then fading into the distance leaving only the lost lonely wail of its whistle and the strong odor of hot oil, cinders and heavy clouds of smoke.

For my most unforgettable adventures, I thank Carlton E. Morse for *I Love a Mystery,* the larger than life adventures of three soldiers of fortune—Jack Packard, Doc Long and Reggie York—investigating reports of werewolves or trying to solve a series of grisly slasher murders usually in creepy old mansions. I ran with my heroes chased by the werewolves and found ourselves locked in wet, moss covered creepy old mansions. It was all real. Carlton E. Morris was one hell of a storyteller and I met him on the radio—the theater of the mind.

In those early years listening to radio drama, sports play-by-play, and the music, I started to wonder if I could possibly become a part of this exciting world called radio. I kept the idea fixed firmly in my mind.

When I followed Edward R. Murrow on CBS to blacked out London, I walked the crowded streets, stood in queues shoulder to shoulder with hungry Londoners, and huddled in underground shelters when bombs and rockets fell, felt the fear and saw the bravery of the British. It was as if I'd been there before.

Music in the Night

My dreams *have* come true. I'm now part of this make-believe world called radio.

Another weekend stretches ahead—Friday evening a bittersweet night for most of those who call. I think I could write a book about lonely women. Weekends and holidays are the hardest they say.

My music is pulled with most of the requests I'm sure they'll be making. Cards and letters, a few notes and a piece of poetry or two are neatly stacked on the console.

Sitting in my chair between the turntables, I hear the faint chattering of the Associated Press news wire. Old man Largen has been true to his word—Fayetteville's new station sparkles with an expensive Raytheon transmitter, two expertly balanced turntables, a new Gates console, and the latest development, a wire recorder.

I let my theme song, *Moonlight Serenade,* play almost all the way through, then without opening the mike or saying a word, I segue to Duke Ellington's *Take the "A" Train.*

Another night has begun. Every show is an adventure. Much the same yet completely different just as every story is different. And tonight like every Friday night she will call, the woman with the husky voice. She will talk, I will listen. I don't even know her name nor do I want to know. Would she share these intimate personal stories with anyone else, even a close friend? I don't think so. Maybe I'm her *only* friend. Maybe in her mind I'm somehow part of the music—beats me. I immediately recognize the voice, "I get so lonely when night comes," she says, "and I need to be with someone . . . we didn't do much but he used to just be here. Sometimes I feel so lonesome I just have to get out. I have a car so I drive around a little. I generally eat dinner late at night . . . God, I so hate to eat alone."

I just listen. No one is asking for an opinion much less advice, that's for sure. My music in the night show is working because I've learned to just keep my mouth shut and play the music . . . their music—music in the night—music to be with, they call it.

I'm as caught up in its mystery and romance as anyone else. Doris Day's *Sentimental Journey* with Les Brown's band breaks my heart every time I hear it. I'm immediately back in Berlin where I heard it for the first time on Armed Forces Radio, so homesick I ache. Homesick for home. Homesick to stay where I am. Sounds crazy, how can a song reach into hearts to pull us back sometimes to places we'd rather forget?

The music I play is heavy with memory of the war years especially for the GIs and their loved ones waiting at home. This music from 1939–1945 I'm sure will never grow old. How could anyone ever forget, Hogey Carmichael's *Stardust* or Major Glenn Miller's *Moonlight Serenade*?

Night after night I take requests and play the music. Long after I turn out the lights, shut the station down, lock the door and walk home, the telephone and the voices are still ringing in my head.

Some of these songs take me back to the Airborne school at Fort Benning and the radio stations at Columbus, Georgia. I was pretty sure then that I'd found my life's work if somehow I could be so lucky. Now it's happening. I feel like my grandfather must have felt long ago when he stood on the stage in full lantern-light playing his fiddle, trying to catch the attention of the young girl he loved. I can't play a fiddle; my stage is a control room doing a nighttime radio show. I take the requests and play the music.

Almost every night I wait for the call that doesn't happen. Tomorrow when Ellen comes to work, I'll say . . . "El, I played your song again last night. Why didn't you call?"

Tomorrow and every Saturday morning for a while I'll be work-

Mike Freeland with Ernest Tucker and Henrietta (the chicken)
in WEKR control room for the Morning Show.

ing an extra few hours with Tucker on his sold out Howdy Neighbor Show, but at this exact moment I can't keep from thinking of a
certain brown-eyed receptionist who is driving me out of my mind.
I know she's kidding but why doesn't she call? But then maybe she's
not kidding. Okay, I'm out of here and that for sure would be best for
her. This innocent barely out of high school kid with a fractured old
soldier—I don't think so. Tonight will not be a good night for sleeping. It's late, I need to settle down. I have an early call for tomorrow
and a busy day.

It's Saturday morning, 5:30 bright and early. I'm at the radio
station. I smell cigarette smoke and the aroma of brewing coffee. I hear Tucker banging around in the transmitter room talking to himself—or talking to the transmitter for all I know. Ernest

From left to right: Melba Chick, Ellen Elmore, Grovene Tucker

(George) Tucker is a popular hometown boy, a fiddle player and a radio man with a radio shop over Carter's Drugs where he repairs radios and publishes songs on the side. Tucker probably knows more about the mechanics of radio than Sarnoff himself. A few people are lucky enough to find their true calling early in life. Tucker is one of them.

Morning radio is a different kind of animal. A work mule, starting the day: Swap and Shop, Trading Post, national news from Mutual network, local news and weather, lost dogs and obituaries, but not enough time for reading all of the mail on the air, hardly time for the music. I see these most requested 78s set aside ready to go. Hank Williams *Cold, Cold Heart*, Patsy Cline's *Crazy*, Jim Reeves *Four Walls*. These tear your heart out songs can be played night or day. God willing these songs will last forever. If I should ever die, play these at my funeral.

Wedding night, November 30, 1948.

The year is 1948, a year history will remember. Congress passed the Foreign Assistance Act, setting up the economic cooperation administration (Marshall Plan) for the rehabilitation of Europe and China.

The military draft came back when Congress passed the Selective Service Act.

The Senate unanimously approved the State Department request for additional funds to expand the "Voice of America" radio programs that are beamed abroad to counteract worldwide anti-American propaganda of the Soviet Union.

The House Un-American Activities Committee reported that its agents had found microfilm copies of " documents of tremendous importance" which had been removed from state department files and given to Russian communist agents. The microfilms were found in a hollowed out pumpkin on the farm of Whitaker Chambers, New York magazine editor who previously had accused Alger Hiss, former state department official of passing the documents to him. Hiss was later convicted of perjury and sentenced to five to ten years in prison.

And at Marr's Café, the pool halls and other places where men gather over coffee to talk sports and solve the world's problems the talk is all about the communist threat and speculation about the next big war sure to come. Most say if it *does* happen it could be the last war.

Ellen and I will remember late fall (November 30) 1948 for a personal and particular reason. Shortly past 8 p.m. on a clear star-filled night at her home at the bottom of a winding gravel road, we stood together holding hands and made promises and vows to each other. We began our life together.

The War Years

January 27, 2009, Kentucky officials report 30 deaths due to storm related causes. Some 101 counties and 75 cities have been declared states of emergency. Soon the entire state, blanketed with snow and ice, will be declared an emergency.

The time is a few minutes before 6 a.m., the best time of day for my walking and meditating, but this morning's quiet is broken by the crash of falling trees and snapping limbs heavy with ice and snow. I'm remembering 65 years ago when sounds like these could have meant certain death—the sounds of German artillery and rifle fire.

Nature's surprise attack sneaked in much like the counter offensive the Germans launched in 1944 through the Siegfried line near Aachen, Germany. Today's weather and scenery is a perfect canvas for that long ago winter war—the eerie quiet, lead gray skies . . . the sound of breaking limbs and crashing trees burdened with snow and ice.

Yesterday has come again. In memory I'm slowly moving through the frozen snow-covered Huertgen forest somewhere south of Aachen, Germany. These dark woods are infested with mines, trip wires and snipers. I jump at the sound of each crack of rifle shot, the crash of incoming German artillery.

My face, feet, and hands no longer ache, they're just numb. Not a good sign. I'm in my medical jeep. In a little while I'll be back at the aid station, long enough to grab some hot coffee and thaw out a minute or so before another run, but how about these poor bastards who have spent the night huddled in fox holes trying to stay alive in icy sub-zero temperatures. Their feet are wet and cold. The threat of frostbite and gangrene are feared almost as much as German bullets.

Every day is one more gift and special. This one indeed does carry me back to yesterday. Yet my mind is confused, spinning this way and that. I'm lost without my journal to remind me, "yes, this is the place, the river, the time and you were there."

I walk on by the silent dark houses near the shallow lake and great oaks through absolute quiet except for the artillery and the sniper.

I joined the 82nd Airborne at Sissone France only a few weeks before it was recalled into battle. At that time the Division was resting, licking its wounds and taking on replacements to fill gaping holes after leaving Holland, nine weeks of a failed campaign leaving behind 800 graves marked by white crosses . . . I'm thinking of Sissone—the so-called rest camp winter of 1944—the sucking yellow-mud streets, the cold slashing rain and sleet turning to snow. Sissone, a drab stony village near Rheims, France, the hard cold, the rumors, the excitement, the wonder.

Today only a handful of 82nd and 101st paratroopers are alive to remember the wild truck ride to meet the German breakthrough, stopping for nothing. The lights flashing on the horizon, the dull rumble of gunfire from the east. None of us will ever forget that campaign (now called the Battle of the Bulge), the agony of the raw cold, the fear.

My scarred brown journal reminds me: *Tonight (this morning) I'm thankful to bed down in a filthy turnip cellar with four other exhausted troopers, and I thank God. Yesterday I drove my medic jeep among and beyond the front lines. We're on the outskirts of the Siegfried Line. Nightmares and horrors of war. My buddy, Mississippi was with me and had to be evacuated in less than an hour. Crazy, calling for his mother. "Momma, where are you? Momma, come and get me!"*

General James J. Gavin

In General Gavin's memoir *On to Berlin* the General speaks of his own nightmare:

> I proceeded on down the trail on foot . . . all along the sides of the trail there were many dead bodies, their gangrenous, broken and torn bodies were rigid and grotesque. Some of them with arms skyward, seemingly in supplication. Nearby were dozens of litter cases, the bodies long dead. Apparently an aid station had been established near the creek and in the midst of the fighting, it had been abandoned, many of the men dying on the stretchers . . .
>
> The sun was setting and I was anxious to get back to the other side of the valley before darkness. As darkness descended over the canyon, it was an eerie scene, like some-

thing from the lower level of Dante's *Inferno*. To add to the horrors, a plaintive voice could be heard from the woods some distance away.

I remember vividly a young soldier; a new replacement was looking with horror at the dead. He began to turn pale, then green and he was obviously about to vomit . . . I knew his state of mind. Every young soldier first entering combat is horrified by the sight of dead bodies that have been abandoned for some time.

My thoughts are of the GI from Mississippi, my medic buddy, a green replacement as I was, up front with the 504 rifle squad. Mississippi, an elite trooper, lost his mind in less than one hour. I hear him today crying for his mother, *"Momma, where are you? Come get me. I'm afraid."*

Somewhere out there an invisible sniper waits. His favorite target is the medic's Red Cross armband, the red cross on the helmet, jeep, or ambulance. Kill the medic and you've crippled more than one. You've harmed the whole unit that he serves. A sniper's rifle can strike greater terror than the rumblings of an approaching Tiger tank. At least you can see and hear the tank.

On my left in a small field among the shorn trees, German snipers lurk. Even before I hear the rifle crack I know my buddy has been hit. He throws down his rifle and helmet, staggers toward me holding his throat with both hands that cannot hold back the spurting stream of bright red blood.

The morning is growing late. Another day is breaking under heavy gray skies. I walk on toward Little River in safe, innocent Hopkinsville, surrounded by the sound of breaking limbs, falling trees, and the bitter cold.

Aachen was the first place the Allies penetrated German soil. The Germans dug in and fought for their motherland with a fanatical resistance. The fighting, with heavy casualties on both sides, raged street to street, house to house, often room to room. At this time I was a member of the 22nd Hospital Train evacuating casualties back to the General Hospital in Paris.

The 82nd Airborne Division, still awaiting reinforcements and re-supply at its base camps in the general area of Rheims, France, moved 110 miles with its first combat elements going into position in less than twenty-four hours and the entire division closing in a new combat area in less than forty hours from the time of the initial alert.

It fought, stopped and held against the best divisions the German leader, Field Marshal Von Rundstedt, could pit against it, protecting the North shoulder of the Allied line, preventing the German break-through from turning north to Liege, Belgium, and providing a safe area through which trapped Allied units could withdraw from the break-through area. This it did despite the fact that its lines at times stretched more than 25,000 yards. Then, turning to the offense, the division set the pace for other units, forcing the enemy back through his famous Siegfried Line.

Aachen, November 16, 1944.

Men fought at times with only rifles, grenades and knives against German armor. They fought with only light weapons in waist-deep snow, in blizzards, in near zero temperatures and in areas where heavy forestation and the almost total lack of roads presented problems that only men of stout hearts and iron determination could overcome.

The battles of "The Bulge," ranking on a par with the brightest victories in the Division's history, also proved again that planes and material are important but the most important essential of all is a fighting heart, a will-to-win. To the troopers of the line goes full credit for the brilliant record they made in the name of the 82nd Airborne Division.
—Extracted from General Gavin's personal report
to a War Department historian:

The First Army's blackest days occurred when the German counter-offensive, rolling at its fastest with the Liege as its objective, came within three -miles of Hodges' headquarters.
Then came a report that the 82nd Airborne Division was moving into positions around threatened Spa.
Hodges moved east to Chaudtontaine at 10:30 pm and the First Army Hq. was save as the 82nd swung into action.
—Hal Boyle, Associated Press Correspondent

Winter is over and spring has come again. Far too many seasons have passed unnoticed. Today Ellen and I live in Hopkinsville, Kentucky, with our dogs Callie, a beautiful collie, and JoJo, a waif we found under a bridge. This morning I see the leaves on the white oaks and tulip trees are almost full size. Only yesterday it seems the limbs were spare black branches with sprigs of green at the end. Our yard is hardly more than the size of two basketball courts yet when we moved here eighteen years ago I found room to plant over 100 oak, poplar and walnut seedlings. I've watched them grow and now some stand as tall as a three-story building.

I walk outside to watch the sun slowly find its way through the trees and listen to the day and the birds come awake. But the quiet this morning is broken by the sound of muffled artillery firing from the practice range at Fort Campbell.

On a day like this, 65 years ago in early May 1945, I was witness to one of the last chapters of the war when I saw the German 21st Army surrender to the 82nd Airborne Division. The surrender followed the 82nd assault across the Elbe River early on the morning of April 30.

The Germans came: first the army, then civilians, and finally displaced persons. With the soldiers were many women, mistresses, children, some refugees. Others apparently had lived with the soldiers for a long time. Many walked, some rode in Wehrmacht trucks, tracked vehicles. Some rode in wagons resting on bundles of hay for their horses. The convoy moved on anything with wheels: bicycles, charcoal-burning and gasoline-powered civilian autos, all manner of carts—ox-drawn, hand-drawn, tractor-drawn—kitchen wagons, and ambulances. Many walked until they could walk no more then flung themselves along the roadside until they recovered enough strength to push on.

The defeated army was not flanked by rows of shimmering Swastikas as it once was. On both sides of the road crude, home-

82nd Airborne soldier in No Man's Land

made white flags flew from every house. Roads were jammed almost beyond description. The Germans moved, not as a military body, but as refugees fleeing from certain disaster, fleeing from the Red Army. Only a few days earlier, the sight of these bucket helmets could have meant certain death. Now they come on and on in a strung out convoy. Not as a disciplined army, but as a frightened, disorganized horde running from the Russians. Here they choose to fight no more. Their war is over.

There Will Come Soft Rains (War Time)

There will come soft rains and the smell of the ground,
And swallows circling with their shimmering sound;

And frogs in the pools singing at night,
And wild plum trees in tremulous white;

Robins will wear their feather fire
Whistling their whims on a low fence-wire;

And not one will know of the war, not one
Will care at last when it is done.

Not one would mind, neither bird nor tree
If mankind perished utterly;

And Spring herself, when she woke at dawn,
Would scarcely know that we were gone.

   Sara Teasdale

Memorial Day, 2010

*I speak for these silent ones who are here with
us today only in spirit and memory.*

I glance at my watch—almost 10 a.m. I'm standing in a light drizzle of rain and fog, waiting while the last sad notes of *Taps* hang in the air. I'm holding the damp pages of my speech rolled up in my left hand.

From the podium I see turned up expectant faces, watching, waiting. Men, women, children, a few gray old men—my age—wearing VFW caps and parts of military uniforms with service ribbons. Who are they, what stories do they have to tell? What must they be thinking?

One veteran, wearing a World War II Eisenhower jacket heavy with ribbons and stripes sits alone at the edge of the crowd, slumped in a wheelchair, waving a small American flag.

An estimated thousand to twelve hundred WWII GIs are dying each day. For many this is the last assembly. I'm not up to this duty before me, but who is? Only God knows how combat veterans hate war, the wasted lives, the insanity, the madness. There's no glory in war. There's got to be a better way. But if war must come, America will answer the call.

I will be introduced as one of the greatest generation. If that is true, which I could argue, let it include not just the military but the families left behind who worked, scraped, saved to support the troops.

I stand at the lectern and wait extra moments thinking—this is the face of America . . . Hometown, U.S.A. Here is the source of America's courage, strength, stamina, and the love that pulls warriors home.

I move close to the microphone, adjust it to fit my comfort, speak:

It wasn't Eisenhower who won the war; it wasn't McArthur.
It wasn't Patton who relieved Bastogne. It wasn't Bradley
who took the bridge at Remagen. None of these men did any
of those things and too little has been said about those who
did—the troops themselves, your fathers, uncles, and mothers,
your sons and daughters. World War II—all wars—are won by
common soldiers who do the dirty work of killing and dying.

I use the word soldier to identify all of our military: the army, marines, the air force, the navy, nurse corps, and all of the women's commands. We must also honor the women who went to work in the factories, raised the children, planted victory gardens, wrote letters, put service stars in their windows, prayed . . . and waited for their men to come home. We call these heroes the home front.

I've seen the ugly face of war. Too often, I've tasted my own fear, and I know one hour in combat changes your life forever. I know war is not fair. The young die first and all the heroes are left behind under plain white crosses. Yet if these heroes could speak to you today, they would say, "Don't call me a hero. I was only doing my duty."

I speak for these silent ones who are here with us today only in spirit and memory.

Today—this Memorial Day—we are all family gathered to honor and to celebrate as best we can our dead. Only because these heroes went to war, fought and died are we free. These young men and women—some only in their teens—paid the

Mike Freeland. Photo by Alex Haglund, *Clay County Advocate-Press*, Flora, Illinois.

full price of war with their blood. And because this is so, we still live in the land of the free.

Today and for the rest of our lives, we must remember the cost of freedom

We are free to assemble.

Free to speak,

Free to write,

Free to choose the work we do,

Free to worship or not worship as we choose.

But words are not enough to express our love and appreciation. Words are only empty symbols. Words cannot tell and cannot support the heavy burden, the pain we feel. We must listen to the silence between the words. Listen from the heart.

Come with me to Normandy, to the Normandy American Cemetery, to the cliff overlooking Omaha Beach and the English Channel. The day is June 6, 1944, D Day.

Hear the cannons boom, the rat-a-tat-tat of machine guns, the snap and crack of rifle fire.

Smell the smoke,

Feel the cold,

Taste your own fear,

Listen to the screams—the prayers—the curses.

The awful clash of battle.

Now walk with me in the cemetery at Normandy on the cliff overlooking the English Channel. Walk with me down the rows of simple white crosses that mark the silent graves. Walk with me to the chapel. On one wall these words are inscribed in stone:

This chapel has been erected by the United States of America
In grateful memory of her sons who gave their lives in the landings on
The Normandy beaches and in the liberation of northern France.
Their graves are the permanent and visible symbol of their heroic
Devotion and their sacrifice in the common cause of humanity.

Another inscription reads:

I give unto them eternal life and they shall never perish.
Through the gate of Death may they pass to their joyful
Resurrection.
These endured all and gave all that justice among nations might
prevail
And that mankind might enjoy freedom and inherit peace. Think not
Only upon their passing. Remember the Glory of their Spirit.

In May 2005, I went back to Europe with a small band of WWII comrades, a trip back to yesterday. Again we walked

Omaha Beach, 2005

the beaches, the battlefields, the lonely cemeteries. We talked to the people. One day in Normandy, when we stopped for lunch in a village, I remember the white haired woman who quietly entered the room and said, "Sirs, may I tell you something. I was four years old but I remember it like yesterday. The Germans were everywhere. They stole our food. They abused us. I even remember how they smelled. Nights my family went out and slept in a ditch in the fields to protect ourselves from the planes. I saw two planes fall out of the sky, fire coming from everywhere, from the air and from the water. I'll always remember the night Americans started jumping out of the sky. You could see long streams of fire. The flares lit up the sky like fireworks. When the Americans came, we were free. It's because of you Americans, I stand here a free woman today. I salute you. My family thanks you. I thank you."

Just these few words, for me, were such a powerful statement. How ironic I thought that in our own land, we take our own freedom and our democracy as a matter of course.

On every mile traveled we found remarkable stories. At Bastogne in Belgium on a hill overlooking the little town we discovered the Peace Forest. Children gathered around us, "Come with me," they said. "I'll show you my soldier's tree."

There on the hill we found trees planted and cared for by the children and their families, each tree named in honor of an American GI who died in one of the bloodiest and most crucial battles of WWII.

We can learn from these children. Today and each Memorial Day, we can plant a symbolic tree in honor of a loved one and remember.

Freedom is not free. It is paid for with the sacrifice and blood of our youth.

Bill Mauldin, a young World War II army sergeant and writer said,

Liberty is a living thing, and like all living things it needs nourishment. If you feel something needs saying and don't say it for fear of popular disapproval, you have withered liberty a bit. If you stop another man or woman from saying what he or she feels, the living plant of liberty dies just a bit. Liberty is dissension, it is argument, debate, politics, and the right to live and work where and as you wish. Liberty is the right of a person to be the captain of his soul and destiny. . . . If we lose it, the deaths of those we honor today are meaningless. If we keep it, their graves are honored in spirit. It is the least we can do for them.

Remember freedom can slip away as quietly as morning fog before the rising sun.

God, protect our young men and women who are fighting and dying even today on foreign fields.

God, grant peace to those who have crossed over the endless river. Grant peace to their families who are gathered here. Heal the pain of the wounded, both physical scars and emotional pain. May your love embrace the innocent who suffered . . . civilians on the battlefield and those left behind. May we be bold in bringing together the eternal dream for human kindness and justice.

God, grant our plea for peace, but if battle must come, give us strength and mercy. We give thanks for the ability to pay our respects to those who have gone before us. May we carry their memories forever with dignity and love and grace.

Amen.

So we come here again
To this sacred place
To remember our buddies
It was only yesterday
Yet you still hear the guns
Smell the smoke
Feel the cold
Taste the fear
From yesterday.

Our group of veterans on the 2005 tour at the
Normandy American National Cemetery.

Paris revisited, 2005: Bob Freeman, Mike Freeland, Lindsay Freeman

On Omaha Beach, pictured left to right: Michael Freeland, Bob Lott, Tom Leamon, Robert Bowen, and George Koskimaki. On the 2005 victory trip to Europe to revisit battlefield and cemeteries, one of our members, Robert Bowen, age 91, fell dead at the *Les Invalids Veterans Hospital*, the burial place of Napoleon. The old warrior had made his last victory lap, marched his last mile, heard the dirge of bagpipes and the sad notes of taps. He died in the very city he helped liberate 61 years earlier.

The River Seine, 2005

In Normandy

Summer has come again to a remembered land
Where the lily of the valley blooms,
Meadow larks build nests and sing in the fields
While here on these cold sands, my brothers bled and died.
A soft summer day in early June,
Come with me and I'll show you where Billy died.
See the shadows, the blood, the gore,
Hear the mad guns gone wild,
The wind choked with curses and prayers.
One boy, a virgin still, throws down his rifle and screams.
Still they come in the boats. Look here's the very cliff
Where rangers climbed the ropes.
The enemy shot them down one by one.
Still they climbed.
Now the guns are silent, grown cold, not remembered.
Today children come to play
And build frog houses and castles
In the barren sand.
What year was that? you say.
Where, Normandy?
The silent waves will tell no more.

The barrage balloons patrolling the English Channel made their way from Camp Tyson near my home town, Paris, Tennessee. Camp Tyson was the nation's only World War II training center. The massive quantities of rubber needed to construct the balloons drove up the price of construction to between five and ten thousand dollars each and became a factor in wartime rationing of tires and rubber products.

Pictured left to right: Former Tennessee Governor Gordon Browning, John Latham, Mike Freeland.

At the end of World War II, George Orwell used the term "Cold War" in the essay "You and the Atomic Bomb" contemplating a world living in the shadow of the threat of nuclear war. He warned of a "peace that is no peace."

Citizens were strongly urged to dig and stock "fallout shelters" and schools held drills to teach children to scramble under their desks and cover their heads. Pictured here is the entrance to a fallout shelter where I spent a week underground during a civil defense exercise.

I thought then as I think now, what kind of world would we be living in if we had to exist like moles and teach our children to scramble under desks and cover their heads.

Mike Freeland, age
37, exiting a Cold War
fallout shelter, 1961

Footlocker

A collection of poems, pictures, essays,
and love letters that have survived with me.
It's not the destination but the journey that counts.

IN TIMES OF WAR

Short Mountain

I've been to Short Mountain
And I've been to war.
They're each a bitch,
But in different ways.
I'm a tired old soldier so
I'll speak of war no more.
But Short Mountain's
Something else.
I can only bend and stretch
These words so far.
So come see for yourself.
One full moon night—or one sunset
Will show you what I mean.
Walk all the way to the top.
Breathe the cold fresh air.
Surround yourself
With the mystery near
Low slung purple skies,
Search the clouds long enough,
You'll find the invisible face of God.

Do Not Resuscitate

I sit by your bed and hold your hand
and wonder, do you know I'm here.

Your gasping breath and muted pulse
announce to me that death is near.

I talk to you of pastures green and waterfalls
and angels 'round.

Let go, I say, and run today.
No broken hip to slow you down.

A fleeting smile, a gentle sigh.
Now all is quiet, but your goodbye.

—Marie Beddingfield, combat nurse

Shellshock

His chart stated a diagnosis of schizophrenia.
Day after day, I watched him, locked in his own world.
Often I wondered, what does he see,
Whose voice does he hear as he marches,
March, march, march down the hall.

Then one day I met someone who had known Bill
Way back when.
"Oh, Bill," he said. "Bill was fine until World War II.
It's shellshock," he said. Bill's never been the same.

Shellshock, just the sound of it conjures up pictures of
Blood and pain. I can hear guns and cannons and calls of
Medic, medic, over here. Over here. Hurry!"
I see you, Bill, a look of fear and disbelief upon your face.
You are immobilized by the horror that surrounds you.
You could not fight that day. Bill, your gun remained silent.

You could not fight that day, Bill. But today
You fight that battle over again and again . . .

    —Marie Beddingfield

Pen and ink sketch of Mike Freeland
by one of his patients, Berlin 1945

REMEMBERING FAMILY

AND FRIENDS

Writing is like building a wood box

Go into your shop
And build a plain wood box
As best you can.
Keep on going back
Day by day to make it better.
After a while—
Maybe a long while,
You'll be surprised to find
That your wood box has turned
Into a beautiful cabinet,
Maybe even a piece of art.
That's the way it is with writing
Just keep on keeping on.

Don't tell me,
show me.
Don't write about a river,
Be the river.
The secret of successful writing:
    The right word
    At the right place
    At the right time.
    But most of all, the silence in between.

My maternal grandmother, Annie Estelle Pate Murphy.

A professional photographer could have worked half a day and still not captured the essence and the soul of my grandmother, Annie Estelle Pate Murphy in this picture snapped by my cousin Jane with a simple Kodak Brownie Box camera. Here she stands braced against the wind and the cold in front of a coal-pile holding a prize goose. I study her square determined face, notice again her large calloused hands and remember her amazing strength.

I recall an earlier time when I was three and she got off the train at Puryear. She wore heavy work shoes, a topcoat hanging below her knees and an elegant red scarf draped around her broad shoulders. I thought she was beautiful. She looked at me, smiled and opened her arms, "Come here, boy. I want you to see my train."

Before I Learned to Read

Before I learned to read and love books, I learned
to read woods signs and love nature. I'm sure by the
time I started to school I knew the whereabouts of
every hawk and owl's nest, every fox's den, persim-
mon tree and bee tree in the hollow.

Nature teaches that time is measured only by
the sun and the moon. You cannot rush a season.
Each has its own way—its own story to tell. Spring
brings the smell of new buds, leaves and blossoms,
fresh plowed ground, the music of a million frogs
from the streams and marshes, songs and squawks
of crows, blackbirds, hawks and the rest. Summer
is growing time. Summer passes at its own sweet
pace, allowing crops to ripen as they will. Early
Indian summer and fall is for gathering crops and
apples, cutting wood getting ready for the coming
of the long winter, but fall is sad because like the
colors of the blazing sumacs, yellow maples, and
hickories, it too will slowly but surely fade away.

Ellen, the proud mother with Mick, our first born, late 1951,
standing by our new Classic Studebaker Land Cruiser.

Patricia, Mike and
Mason at the Blood
River Farm, 1984

Ellen at our farm, 1978. During World War II Ellen
served on the home front as courier for the community.
She says "Our telephone served the whole Camargo
community. I remember one spring morning taking a call
for a neighbor and riding my pony Princess two miles to
deliver the dreaded message: Your son has been killed in
action."

Bugs, my constant companion, who
encouraged me in every way he could, but
who never lived to see our finished book.

Mike and Ellen in Italy, October 12, 2006.

A Song for Ada

I'd never seen
My grandfather cry
Until that first time
Under the dark cedars
When he carried wild roses
To Ada's grave.

I saw him sitting there on the red clay ground
Alone and silent
Talking to no one
But himself

I often wonder
What it's like in the long dark night
When he hears her voice calling his name—
Reaching to hold her,
To find only a cold empty place.

I often wonder:
Who do you hold when your love is gone?
Who's to share your life,
And sunsets and dreams
When your love is dead?

The Baptizing

And again they came, that early Sunday morning,
　　A wet-dew August morning,
　　　To beat the heat and prepare the way.

In the shade of the hackberry trees
　　Behind the church where red sumacs grow
　　　We spread the bounty from the fields.

And sang songs with frogs and whippoorwills.
　　"Shall the Circle be Unbroken"
　　　"In the Sweet-by-and-by."

Yonder stands my love,
　　Tall and tan in her wet, white dress.

Come walk with me, love, give me your hand.
　　Follow me deep into the cool water.
　　　There among the ferns,
　　　　　All of your sins, like summer memories,
　　　　　Will be washed away.

I Knew Hank

Left home before good daylight
Heading east toward Greenville
Up State Highway 93 to Kingsport
Out US 23 to Gate City to Big Stone Gap
And Appalachia on the trail of the Lonesome Pine.
On to bloody Harlan, a town lost in purple fog
Song, mystery, coal dust and legend.
Hank Williams rides with me all the way
On the radio. Like we were walking to the sky.

Take Me with You

Take me with you
Wherever the road leads.
If the sun shines hot,
I will be your shade.
When winter comes,
My love will warm you.
Should the road be rough,
My feet will smooth it.
When darkness falls,
I will light a candle.
There will be a hand to hold
If you are afraid.
We will drink the wine of joy,
Eat of ripe fruit,
Pick fragrant lilacs in the spring.
Do not walk the road alone,
Take me with you.

—Betty Grogan, Hopkinsville, Kentucky
friend and fellow writer

Relics

Scattered across our rural countryside they sit,
The old barns,
Rotting quietly,
Relics of the past.
Soon they'll be gone.
Who cares?
Needed no longer.
Not forgotten so much as ignored.
Symbolic of a time when people were part of the land.

The hunter knows.
He walks the old fields with dog and gun.
He knows!
Remember the covey by Reynolds barn?
Remember the footprints in the sand?
Remember sun on a lover's hand?

Maybe,
If we care enough,
It's not too late—
For old dogs,
And old barns,
And old men.

— Charlie W. Owen, New Johnsonville, Tennessee
friend and former student

The old barn stands on land called the Buck Lick, once owned
by Allen Durwood Freeland, my great-grandfather.

Once Upon a Time
for Trish

Once upon a time
When the world was young. Pure. Innocent
A beautiful young princess lived in a haunted old house
By the side of the road.

An old house filled with dusty magic
Many ghosts
Sad-eyed puppies
Calico cats
Pesky little brothers
And frogs of many colors

Every day the young Princess
Kissed the frogs hoping to find her Prince
Until finally, one spring-filled day
Her charming Prince appeared!
Ka-Zam! Just like that... riding a white horse.

Very soon—all too soon
They rode away together to a far land over the mountains,
Across the river
And lived happily ever after.

Now the haunted old house sits alone—silent
Except for the singing winds, slapping shutters
And hushed voices in the night.
The old house remembers.
The old house cannot forget.

Raindrop

Raindrop come
Splash in the puddle with me!
It's pouring, thundering, lightening and wishey-washey
And wet and wet. Oh, Oh, Please don't go.
I'll be lonely without you. Now
It's foggy. A rainbow
Is coming. Look!
Now it's
SUNNY!

—Melissa Poe, age 10

Melissa

Wet north wind chills your name
Like the sound of some strange crippled bird
Croaking its song to a world that died in the night
When no one watched
And few cared.

In this summer hiding-place we played.
Built dreams and frog houses
Sand castles and old songs,
Collecting white shells to hold fragile memories.

Eternity embraced between then and now.
When you smiled—crossed your heart
And pledged your virgin vow.

Do you remember, Melissa?
I've lived with the night
A million years or more
Listening to the wind, whispering your name,
Melissa.

The Old Ford Truck

The old Ford was a mule to say the least. Not
really too pretty to look at, not so easy to get along
with, but strong. The bumpy ride was a part of her
walk. The dents and bruises were not blemishes
on the body, but were like calluses on the hand of
a laborer—each dent telling a story—the entire
truck writing a novel.

I will always remember the faded weathered
cream color of my dad's Ford pick-up. The original
bed had long since been replaced with a flatbed of
wooden boards that my dad hammered together
himself. The doors creaked when you yanked them
open. The seats were falling apart and the blue
plastic that covered the foam was mysteriously
vanishing. The front headlight hung swollen like
the eye of a boxer.

The old Ford had not only countless road miles
but also countless work'en miles. Regular road
miles are put on by the novices but work'en miles
are when you load the back of the truck with cable
and scrap metals so massive that the weight of
the load shoves the bed of the truck down almost
to the ground and the front wheels dangle in the
air—barely holding on to the sharp corners of the
road as the front engine screams for more power
steering fluid. The Ford worked a solid five days

a week. Pulling with all six cylinders against the yoke of the chassis as my father's foot stomped at the throttle carrying scrap metal to the junk yard of Steiner Lift or hauling small loads to different companies around town—the old Ford always pulling more than just its weight.

The truck was a legend among our family and among the neighbors who could hear the rumble as the truck drove the quiet streets. When Dad first

Mason Poe

bought the used truck, the suspension was shot. We always assumed the reason was because the truck was the same one featured in a mid 70's TV commercial—being dropped out of an airplane.

The old Ford was not driven for glamour or attention, though the truck did have a certain eye-catching appeal—like that of a mule at a pony show. The truck was driven for practicality and necessity. The old Ford's beauty was not found in the weathered cream paint that covered the body. The beauty was found in the spirit and in the hard work that put each dent there.

Yesterday the old Ford made her last trip to the scrap yard. Not hauling scrap of her own—but giving the last that she could to this world. Ashes to ashes, rust to rust.

—Mason Poe

Sundays Best

Peach tea
Sweat through the glass
Yams, orange and butterflied
Walnut sprinkled wings
Glazed in clover honey.
Sliced red tomatoes
Dominoed over mashed potatoes
Corn bread broken in half and buttered
Sweet cream of corn
Cut from the cob
Snapped green beans mixed with sweet peas
White beans with white onion spires
And chow-chow poured on the side.

On the back porch
Ross Jr. and I spit cherry pits over the banister.
Grandmother swings in the long porch swing
And looked deep into fields with
Fences withdrawing a weathered ribbon
Rising and falling
In and out of sight
Tapering fine rusty point.
Maw-Mike reads the paper and sleeps
In the once white wicker chair
Used by the cats to sharpen claws.
Grandmother Elmore made sock monkeys.

Skippy, Eastwood, Baby and Bear
Panted, scratched and sometimes smiled.
Clyde, Charlie, and Mac
Stretched, kneaded, yawned,
Looked at flies with disdain and apathy.

Like a child's hand into church
humidity held the day.
Hot weather
Had nothing to do with the breeze;
Or the long shadows
Or lightening bugs
Or crickets
Or bull frogs
Or the bobwhite
Or whippoorwills
Or the next day
Or the day after that
Or even weeks after.
But Sunday's stale heat didn't matter.
Sundays we surrendered and watched life
        with full stomachs.

— Grandson Mason Poe, age 15

Pipe Smoke

You're gone.
The whine of tires is a faint echo.
Now only the frogs
Laughing in perfect compatibility
At my solitude.
There was so much to say,
It remains unsaid.
So much love to show.
But now there is only me
And the frogs
And pipe smoke.
  —Stephen Allen Freeland
  from the year he lived alone at the cabin

Love Song

If love knew where some strangers keep
  Within deep walls an unquiet bird,
Perhaps sometimes into our cage
  That love would watch.

If love knew what some secrets yield;
  The sense, the thrill, the taste of love;
Perhaps sometimes that love would pause
  Before our wall.

If love knew where rich silence steals;
  Disguise her cries (the stolen breath);
Perhaps sometimes that love would wait;
  Bestow her eyes.

If you knew how one loves you true,
  And if you knew how much,
Perhaps sometimes our love would will
  Her gentle touch.

—Stephen Allen Freeland

To My Brothers
Wherever I May Find Them

There was once a time
When we all traveled
Together — tremulously sometimes —
On the same horse.

And a horse it was
Or more often
A motorcycle or
A dump truck or
An air plane . . .

One by one we came
With marked progress
And only a moment's interruption
One, oops, two, three, four

The philosopher, the poet,
The achiever, and the friend
Who were we then, before we were suffused
In these somber hues
Of tomorrow.

We were brothers
One, oops, two, three, four
The philosopher, the poet,
The achiever, and a friend.

Who are we now?
One, oops, two, three, four
Long after the begin did begin.

To my brothers
Wherever I may find them.

—Stephen Allen Freeland

The brothers, left to right, David Elmore, Douglas Lee,
Stephen Allen, Michael R. Jr., 1964.

Beekeeper: The Last Romantic

Wind sings and dances in the leaves
And courts the blossomed apple tree,
Below them you who mates the bee.

About the bees, among the trees
From hives you've built you draw
The sweet drink of the God, And He
In name divine weeps not for all
The monstrous rustling of the leaves.
And what care you, who loves the bee.

—Stephen Allen Freeland
for Grandpa Mason

Song of the Sands

You are at best angels fallen,
Who are not good enough to be
Forever saved, nor bad enough
To be forever lost in
The voiceless fog of Sybil's dream.
You are at worst most sterile things,
Who are not bad enough to be
Forever lost; nor good enough
To be forever chained against
The hopeless fire of Zeus' rock.

—Stephen Allen Freeland

Steve, age 24, with
unknown students at
LaGrange Academy,
LaGrange, Georgia
where he taught French
and literature and
coached Lacrosse

Lillian

Well, I just strolled around
Up to the old home
One Sunday day.

Well, no
That's not so
I came to mow her yard.

Well, I pushed that awkward machine,
Pushed that yellow thing
From the gravel onto her multi flowered lawn.

And then. . . . .
She came from around the back of the house,
A thin small black frame
Cast against white.

"I've come to mow your yard," I said,
Feeling big.

She gave no answer.
It was
Sunday day.

"Or would you wish I wait?" I said
Feeling small.

"You know what the Lord say
About working on a Sunday.
You can if you want to."

I wasn't doing her any favors.
So we sat on the porch.

And talked

She talked,
"The Lord giveth and.
The Lord taketh away."

She said, looking at nothing
And with a lisp
And a weak tremble,
Hiding a sly smile.

—Stephen Allen Freeland

In the Garden

Sirius seethes sour in the mid-afternoon sun.
In the disheveled garden the Johnson grass
Chokes the last of the spring crocuses.
The putrid scorched scent of ragged weeds
And surging wisteria crowd for your attention.
The young wife sitting in her cluttered garden
Stoops into a half-moon gesture—her curved breasts
And thighs turning for the scathed earth—
And gathers a solitary prudent beauty;
The butter cup, or naked lady, covered
By the burning stench of Johnson grass.

—Stephen Allen Freeland

Mother's Day

I could give you flowers,
    Blue, yellow, green or red.
Or I could give you jewelry
To please your heart instead.

I could take you places,
    But what have your eyes not seen?
So, what do I give you?
I give you love and hope and a dream.

I give you my love,
    All for you to keep,
And I give you a dream
    To comfort you as you sleep.
And I give you hope,
Knowing that your goal for me is never to sleep.

You see, Mom, just for you,
    My funds I could easily choke
But all that's meaningless without love.
And, besides, I'm broke.

Happy Mother's Day,
From you biggest fan.
Love, Steve

    —Stephen Allen Freeland

Notes

Dear one,
This has been a long
And lonesome day.
I missed our coffee
And touching you.
If somehow we should
Miss each other today,
Only know I love you
And long to be with you.

My life is filled
With joyous memories
Of times we've shared
Of shells we've found,
Treasure more precious
Than gold.
I cherish each moment
But none more
Than now.

—Ellen Freeland

Christmas Is

Christmas is
The smell of the cedar tree, new cut and fresh,
The taste of tangerines, sweet and tangy,
The sound of familiar voices singing Silent Night
In a quiet country church
The feel of an open fire,
The glisten of paper icicles sparkling in the glow of the fire,
And most of all
The joy of friends and family, who make life special,
You who mean so much to me.
 Merry Christmas and Happy New Year.

—Ellen Freeland

SELECTED POEMS
OF MICHAEL FREELAND

The old cabin still stands and looks much like it did in 1926. Mom and Dad, my grandfather Pap, and Uncle Hall built the cabin and side room from an abandoned Wilson cabin with logs even then believed to be about 100 years old.

Christmas at Home

I write you these lines from our home place,
the place where I was born and raised,
a one room log cabin on the creek bank
at the head of Wilson Holler.

I know every rock and tree and hill,
And why the red sumacs bloom.
I know where wild grapes grow
And where chicken hawks hide their nests.

And I know when a mockingbird sings in December,
God is near.
Last night outside my window there was a heavenly chorus!
I come here again, as every season,
to feed the birds
and to heal my soul.

Tomorrow, as fresh as new snow,
Christmas comes again to Wilson Holler.
So, tonight by my fire,
Listening to songs of mockingbirds
I send you this wish for joy and peace
and all the magic of Christmas.

My Love

Was there ever in all of time
A day like this? Just so:
Of all the other times
And all the other places
Will you remember . . .
Our last time?

Will you remember candlelight,
The taste of warm wine
The laughter and the tears,
The silence in between,
Will you not remember . . .
My name?

The Land

The land speaks to the soul:
The silence and smell of woods
After rain.
And the way the sky looks
At sunset
Or break of day.
Spring's first frogs singing
In the marshes.
The clear call of bobwhites.
The morning dove.
You can keep all of your creeds.
Keep them all.
One walk in the woods
Or by the river
Is enough for me.

The Wind

Dark comes early to my cabin
And a heavy quiet
As often happens before the coming storm
And in battle.
An early full moon hangs
Just out of reach
On the hill
Waiting
For the rockets to fall
Waiting and watching.
Tanks rumble in the distance,
Artillery streaks the far-sky.
And I wait
Surrounded by now
But wrapped in yesterday.
I am alone except for
The cries of the dying
And the careless wind
Talking to the trees.
The wind does not remember.
The wind does not care.

The Sound of Silence

In the hush
Of morning
In a warm valley
Called forget the sun.

In a gentle field
Surrounded by horizon
Quick night birds
And war gods,
She found peace
And forgiveness
And a perfect place to die.

"Forgive me, God," she said.
And that was all
Except for the cries of night birds
And the sound of silence.

Poetry Is

"You want poetry?"
The old man asked.
"Write your own, ain't
No poetry police
Keeping you from it.
One thing to remember, though—
Poetry is
What it is
Nothing less
Nothing more.
Poetry speaks for itself if you'll only listen.
It is the sound of rushing water
When the river is high
Sounds of trains leaving in the night
Through tunnels of smoke and purple fog.
Long dark trains filled with faceless people
And what might have been.
That's what poetry is
Or ought to be."

Someday

Someday
I'll come again
and write a poem about September,
not a tired song of lazy Indian summer days
or turning leaves dancing in the wind.

Let me write an honest poem
telling of our love
warm red wine
and the timeless magic of candlelight.

Someday
when you are gone
I'll come here again
in the deep night
to light candles
and remember September.

In the Valley of Yesterday

To this haunted place I return
To our valley of yesterday
Where we knew love and wildflowers
Black-eyed Susan's and the summer rose.

In this valley, before I rest
And sleep among the pines
Come again and hold me
Hold tight sweet memories, dead
Like winter's lilac,
Crushed like summer's rose.

Michael Mason Rudolph Freeland,
age 14

We Are One

I'm awake before good light
To hear the world come alive:
The thrill of katydids and whippoorwills
And owls.
One owl calls from
Down the hollow.
Soon one answers
From the hill.
These songs I love
But the silence more

Come be with me
Let me hold your hand
Forever.
We are one.

Today I will be content
With few words
Only today
Let me learn
From the sound
Of tumbling waters.
The traveling wind
And the awareness
Of now.

I Am My Dog's Best Friend

I talk and Callie listens—
Or pretends, I can't be sure.
Sometimes I believe she reads my mind.
I say I am her master
She knows better but we both pretend.
So it is with love, I think.
Is it real—or pretend?
You never know until it's over.
Then you wonder—is it really over?
Callie and I walk on toward a full summer moon
And watch it disappear behind a cloud.
The night has turned dark, lost, empty
Like lost love when it goes away.

October's Girl

Before this scarlet sun sets
    Behind these dark hills
        I number again
      Endless days.
Anniversaries are sand prints
    That come as silent
        as field mice
            in the night
down a quite path lost somewhere
    at the end of a summer rain.
So sing your song, October morning.
These October hills know it well,
    Telling the world of a special gift,
      October's brown-eyed girl.

The Sacred Kitchen: Forbidden Fruit

Forgive me, Father, for I have sinned.
But in truth, Father, the woman made me do it,
With chocolate, black dreamy, full bodied.
The woman tempted me,
Her name is Chocolata.
Once upon a soft August morning
I was captured by the sweetness
Of her smile,
Her hard embrace,
Her panache (or is that the word for chocolate flavor?)

Deliver me, Father, from the temptation
Of this garden. Snakes and apples I can handle,
But the smell, the touch, the
Taste of chocolate
Is more than I can bear.
    (In the year of Chocolate, 2009
    John C. Campbell Folk School)

Afterwards

Afterwards
You turned away
To a place beyond my touch
As though we had never been here before
Or walked together in the rain,
Or watched early breaking light
Celebrate the coming day.

We dressed without talking
Then drove until two lanes became one
And the one gave way to
A ribboned path of white sand and shells.

I remember that cloudless day
The taste and smell of sun, sand and sea
And I am forever lost in its time and wonder
As I now walk alone
In places we've never been.

February Winds

February winds play games of hide-and-seek
with small black clouds that scurry
to find the amber sun,
casting shadows that etch memories
of a pig-tailed, brown-eyed girl,
holding still, two dolls, Hortense and George,
a calico cat and a wildflower.

Now she sings a love song to her first born
and whispers secrets that she learned
from an old house that sits silent
and listens to the February wind.

Tom Buchanan

Tom Buchanan, Martha's youngest,
rode his little red mare home from the big war
singing all the way.
Big handsome man, liked women,
good times and sour mash whiskey.
(Women liked him, too.)

They say one night that spring, Tom went to a dance
and didn't come home.
Martha woke from a dream seein' Tom's little
red mare standin' under the cedars
shiverin' wet, muddy, head hanging down,
Saddle under her belly.

Martha got out of her bed, walked the floor til daylight
"I seen Tom. Tom's drowned in Bloody River!"
When daylight came, she looked and there under
the trees stood the little red mare. Wet. Muddy.
Just like in her dream.

Tom sleeps now and will evermore under old cedars
near the river, where restless winds moan in the trees.
Some say every spring on full moon nights when
the river is wild and high, a little red mare comes and
waits by his grave.

Blood River

I'm leaving in a couple of
hours, hitchhiking
to Blood River to get away
from the cable news.
However if the sky falls, I
expect to be one
of the last old coyotes left
standing. Presently
(Thank the Lord) I have a mate who
promises to be
at my side. Realistically
you know how that is:
Let the first coyote show up
in a new set of
wheels with the top down and music
on the radio
and there goes your dream. Anyway,
I have enough good
judgment left to follow my dad's
advice. "Son, go as
far back in the hills as you can
on a little piece
of land and stay away from the
government." So this
little piece of land is so far
off the beaten path
I can drink fresh running water
Out of my cupped hands.

This rail fence, split from red or white oak logs, is typical of those used in the 1800s. These were brought to our farm from Lincoln County, Tennessee by my father-in-law, Tom Elmore.

Shadows

I hide in the empty shadows
Alone
Invisible
Not remembered

Dancing flames shoot sparks of fireflies
While the old ones
Tell the old stories
One more time.

I watch as the hungry fire
Brands pictures in my mind.
Outside the howling wind wraps its fingers
Around the cold black night.

Epilogue

Freeland Family History

The English family name Freeland is classified as being of habitation origin, in other words, those family names which find their origin in the location of the residence of the first known bearer. Freeland is derived from two Old English words meaning "free land," denoting "one who held land free of rent or feudal obligation."

One of the earliest references to this name or to a variant is a record of Walter Friland who is listed in the Feet of Fines in County Norfolk in 1188. Humphrey Freeland and Agnes Styles obtained a marriage license in London in 1595. This name was introduced to America as early as 1677 when Isaac Freeland emigrated and sailed to Maryland.

MARKER NO. 506-9

Davidson Co., Nashville, 1400 – 8th Ave. N.

Freeland's Station

On this site stood one of the principal stations of the
Cumberland Settlements. Felix Robertson, son of
Col. James Robertson and the first white child born
in the Settlement, was born here, January 11, 1781.
On January 15 the fort was attacked by Indians,
who were repulsed and driven westward.

James Dunn Freeland was born in 1730 in Scotland or Ireland and died in 1807 in Orange County (now Alamance), North Carolina. He was married to Elizabeth and had two sons, James D. Jr. and Thomas.

James D. Freeland, Jr. was born in Orange County, North Carolina in 1755. He fought in the Revolutionary War and is listed in Captain Bledsoe's Roster of 1777. (White's Kings Mountain Men). He was married to Sarah Dinwiddie of North Carolina. James Jr. moved his family to Maury County, Tennessee before 1810 and settled in Mooresville. The land on which Mooresville is located is part of North Carolina Land Grant No 87.

The children of James D. and Sarah Freeland were James D. III, John, Joseph, Thomas, William, Sarah, Rebecca, and Robert Daniel.

Robert Daniel Freeland was born April 6, 1798, in Orange County, North Carolina, and was married to Ann Mariah Headen on October 25, 1823 in Maury County, Tennessee. Their children were Allen Durwood, Mary Jane, Constantine, Amanda E., Horton, and Maria A.

James died before 1820, Sarah in 1836. James and Sarah are buried in a family cemetery located on the farm in Maury County.

Robert sold his farm in 1842 because of a business venture that went sour. He had been in business in Mooresville with Joseph W. Calvert when the "crash of 1837" came. Robert experienced financial setbacks in the next several years. In 1841 he had still not been able to settle all claims against him. He heard that hogs were bringing a premium price in Mobile, Alabama, and decided to drive hogs to Mobile to recover his fortune. In the fall of 1841, he and his brother, Thomas, purchased a herd of 800 hogs from all over Marshall County and began the drive. With no cash, they gave notes to each individual from whom they purchased hogs, and then borrowed money to pay hands to help them on the drive. On the way south they gave notes for hog feed, food and lodging, and other expenses. On the way back they paid off the notes with the exception of a note in the amount of $386 to Leonard Twitty. Twitty had sold them the largest number of hogs and sued Robert to recover on the debt. Robert's financial difficulties increased forcing him to sell his 569 acres of land at Bear Creek and he and his wife, Ann Mariah,

The John W. Freeland Family on the porch of the family home, 1897.
Left to right: Ada holding Lettye, Maude, Cordelia, and John

along with his brother Thomas and sister-in-law, Jane, moved their families to Carroll County, Tennessee to begin a new life.

The 1850 census shows the Freeland brothers and their families had moved again now settled in Henry County near Buchanan where they built a gristmill, general store, and lodging house. Buchanan is located in the northeast section of Henry County and was settled in the early 1840s. It was named after the then president of the United States, James Buchanan. One unit of the confederate cavalry was organized by General Nathan Bedford Forest in the shade of a large oak tree that stood on the present campus of Buchanan school.

Robert's son Allen Durwood Freeland married Margaret Buchanan. Their son, John Wesley Freeland (October 9, 1859–June 20, 1945) was "Pap," my grandfather. Pap married Ada Sally Ray and they had five daughters: Cordie May Verdell (Wayne), Maude

The Freeland Family 1964. Left to right: Douglas Lee Freeland, Ellen Freeland holding David Elmore Freeland, Stephen Allen Freeland, Michael R. Freeland, Jr., Mike Freeland, and Patricia Sharon Freeland

Grubbs (Curg), Lettye Forcie Sykes (Cordell), Ozella Ray Wisehart (Harris), and Henda Love Grubbs (William); and two sons: Hall Allen Freeland and Mason Noel Freeland, my father.]

Mason Noel Freeland (1904–1988) was married to Wilby Lee Murphy (1904–1960). Their children were Michael (Mason) Rudolph (born May 14, 1924), Randolph Noel (October 2, 1930), Jamie Walvin (September 4,1939), and Eva Lane (October 28, 1944).

Michael Rudolph Freeland and Flora Ellen Elmore were married on November 30, 1948.

The Will of Robert Daniel Freeland, April 1, 1868

Recorded in Henry County
Book of Inventories of Wills, page 581.

I Robert D. Freeland, Compos Mentis, do declare the following to be my last will and testament.

1st, I want all my just debts paid out of the means on hand before any other distribution is made.

2nd, I give to my wife, K. E. Freeland all my property, real and personal (with such exceptions as may be hereafter made) to be used for her benefit and my four younger children until the youngest shall attain to the age of sixteen years at which time I desire and will that the same shall be sold and proceeds of the same to be equally divided among my wife, my daughters Amanda E. Buchanan and Maria A. Purcell, my son Albert Sidney Freeland and my daughters Martha Davis Freeland and Laura E. Freeland.

3rd, I give to my son John James Freeland one half of my grist mill. The other half to be appropriated for the benefit of my family until the youngest is sixteen years old after which time, John James, my son, is to have all of the mill with seventy-five acres of land adjoining the same that which is most convenient for a mill site.

4th, I bequeath to my daughter Emily Matilda Cowden the sum of one dollar to be paid by my Executor out of any means on hand.

5th, I bequeath to my son Allen D. Freeland three hundred dollars excepting so much as he is owing me by note or account.

6th, I bequeath to my daughter Mary Jane Weaver the sum of one dollar.

7th, I give to my daughter Amanda E. Buchanan five hundred dollars of such means as effects of mine as shall be on hand.

8th, I give and bequeath to my daughter Maria Angeline Purcell the sum of five hundred dollars. These several sums for my children to be collected and paid as soon as practical by my executor.

9th, I give my son John James a horse and saddle.

10th, I appoint my son-in-law, George Buchanan, as my Executor of this my last will. In testimony whereof I have hereunto set my hand and seal this the first day of April, AD 1868.